CHINA:
A RISING GLOBAL POWER

CHINA:
A RISING GLOBAL POWER

A Historical and current Perspective /
analysis of Modern Day China

RICHARD DE LON

PARTRIDGE

To order additional copies of this book, contact
Toll Free +65 3165 7531 (Singapore)
Toll Free +60 3 3099 4412 (Malaysia)
orders.singapore@partridgepublishing.com

www.partridgepublishing.com/singapore

This book is dedicated to my parents

Lionel Teo Peng Chong

&

Lee Soh Hua

Who have always been my inspiration

CONTENTS

The Uyghur Issue 1

Hong Kong Security Law 10

India vs. China 21

Quad Alliance 25

The Eurasia Times 29

China and Pakistan 31

China and Philippines 34

China and Vietnam 37

China and Thailand 41

China and Malaysia 43

China and South Korea 46

China and Japan 49

China and Indonesia 53

China vs. Australia 58

China and United Kingdom 68

China and Taiwan 75

The Death of US Reserve Currency 79

China's Strategy to Deflect Western Hostility 86

Will US and China Go To War? 89

US and Other Countries Decoupling from China 100

Covid-19 from Wuhan, The Pandemic 104

The Imminent Collapse of The American Empire 108

The Future of China 113

China's early history is replete with incidents of barbarians crossing its borders and pillage to raid and rob the villages bordering Mongolia. Emperor Qin Shi Huang (220–206 BC), the first emperor of China, came up with the grandiose plan to build the Great Wall of China to prevent the invaders (various nomadic groups from the steppes) from crossing into the border. Subsequently, successful dynasties continued to build and lengthen stretches of the border walls. It was, however, during the Ming Dynasty (1368–1644) that many of the main stretches of the wall were built and maintained during this era. The purpose and functions of the wall are better described by Wikipedia as follows:

> "Apart from defense, other purposes of the Great Wall have included border controls, allowing the imposition of duties on goods transported along the Silk road, regulation or encouragement of trade and the control of immigration and emigration. Furthermore, the defensive characteristics of the Great Wall were enhanced by the construction of watchtowers, troop barracks, garrison stations signalling capabilities through the means of smoke or fire, and the fact that the path of the Great Wall also served as a transportation corridor."

The study and understanding of China's early history seek to comprehend the minds of early Chinese thinking. They were fearful of foreign invaders coming into China and that led to the building of the wall. It, therefore, dispels any notion of China to invade or colonize any neighboring territories. In short, the early Chinese dynasties did not harbor or possess any intention to invade, conquer, or annex any territories neighboring their middle kingdom.

During the early Ming Dynasty, Zeng He (1371–1433) whose original name was Ma He, a mariner, and a Muslim during the Emperor Yongle, commanded expeditionary treasure voyages to Southeast Asia, the Indian subcontinent, Western Asia, and East Africa from 1405 to 1433. The ships with multiple decks carried hundreds of soldiers and were twice as large as any wooden ships ever recorded during those times. At that time and era, Admiral Zeng He commanded a fearsome armada of ships that sailed to those ports. The purpose of this revelation is to show that even during this period of Chinese rule in the fifteenth century, the Chinese had no ambitions to conquer or colonize any of the countries he visited or traded. Instead through these voyages, he forged a lot of goodwill missions in the Asian archipelago.

These two early revelations in the history of China clearly demonstrated the view that China never had any territorial ambitions to conquer, colonize, or annex any of those territories it had landed to trade.

A WESTERN PERSPECTIVE OF CHINA

US and Western propaganda have been very active in promoting China as a totalitarian communist country hell-bent on global hegemony. The narrative by Western media has consistently painted China as being aggressively pursuing superiority both economically and militarily. Its Belt and Road Initiative has been labeled as a debt trap to secure the host country's influence. Such narrative, however, has not received much traction among 170 countries that participated in the Belt and Road Initiative. Stretching from China's province of Xinjiang across Russia and reaching the EU states, the result has been phenomenal. Trade among the countries involved in the BRI has increased many folds and, without a doubt, benefitted those participating countries.

US behavior toward China can be described as strange and inconsistent with the principles of international relations. It has always been critical of other countries interfering in their affairs, yet they display no constraint in interfering in other countries' affairs. The interference even extends to passing various bills directing in the internal affairs of China. The Uyghur Human Rights Policy passed by the US House would target Chinese officials. The legislation would ensure the assets of the Chinese would be frozen and their entry to the US would be barred (see article below).

The other Senate legislation was the Hong Kong Autonomy Act which seeks to sanction Beijing and Hong Kong officials (see article below). How would US feel if China was to pass similar bills targeting US human rights record with the Black minority? And what about their abysmal treatment of immigrants at the Mexican border? Also not forgetting their immigration discrimination against Muslims from certain Muslim countries? And their treatment of Muslim ISIS in Guantanamo Bay has been most degrading. So their criticisms of Chinese treatment of Uyghurs in Xinjiang is sheer hypocrisy. Since when have they been concerned about the human rights of their own Black minority?

The whole act of criticizing China for introducing the Security Laws in Hong Kong and the treatment of Muslim Uyghurs in Xinjiang have all been part of the grand design of demonizing China with the ultimate aim of destabilizing China. It is common knowledge that CIA operatives using the National Endowment of Democracy (NED) has been supporting Uyghur radicals to demand an independent Xinjiang province. It was the violent acts of these radicals that prompted China to put them in educational camps to deradicalize them. The US attempt to encourage the Uyghurs to have an independent state was to put a spanner in the Belt and Road Initiative. The Xinjiang Province which provides a vital link for the Belt and Road Initiative to Russia and Europe to the European states would virtually collapse with an Independent Xinjiang. Any attempt to make this resource-rich province to be independent would be futile as the Uyghurs only make up 40 percent of the population in Xinjiang.

The US and Western media has often claimed that one million of the Uyghurs population were incarcerated in concentration camps. This common narrative was perpetuated by the so-called "World Uyghur Congress" funded and supported by the US government through their NGO, National Endowment of Democracy (NED). However, no Muslim country is buying the "concentration camps" narrative. Turkey, which is closest to Uyghur (of Turkic Origin), came to China some time ago and reiterated that the Uyghur reeducation centers would not affect China-Turkey relations.

In order to further refute the lies about Xinjiang, I would like to quote a statement made by the Organisation of Islamic Cooperation (OIC) with fifty-six Islamic member countries after a visit to Xinjiang in March 2019.

"The council welcomes the outcomes of the visit conducted by the General Secretariat's delegation upon invitation from the People's Republic of China: commends the efforts of the People's Republic of China in providing care to its Muslim citizens: and looks forward to furthering cooperation between the OIC and the People's Republic of China."

The Western imperialists, especially the US and the UK, would like to see Xinjiang in turmoil. They would like to see Xinjiang revert to an independent country that is controlled by the US. The ultimate aim was to sever China's access to Central Asia, Russia, and Europe, thus slowing China's economic growth.

XINJIANG AND UYGHURS—US AND WESTERN NARRATIVES DEBUNKED

The favorite theme narrated by US and Western media is that there are "1 million Uyghur Muslims in concentration camps," ethnic cleansing, and cultural genocide. Now where did the 1 million detained Uyghur number come from? During the World Uyghur Congress, Chairman Omer Kanat was asked by Max Blumenthal, an American journalist, and the only answer he could provide was that it was only a Western media estimate. This Western media estimate, which has often been quoted by bipartisan lawmakers in America, resulted in the formulation of the UYGHUR Human Rights Policy Act.

This act sanctions Chinese officials over Xinjiang camps and also prohibits the export of goods and services in the region where the supposedly Uyghurs were being held. Two things need clarification here. The World Uyghur Congress is sponsored by an American so-called NGO, NED (National Endowment for Democracy), which is a CIA operative. The US had used the Uyghur issue to instigate them to be rebels or terrorists. And in doing so would encourage them to fight for "independence" and in doing so would ultimately sabotage the BRI (Belt and Road Initiative). The result would be to ensure that the global project would end in failure.

The Uyghur Human Rights Policy Act is a reflection of sheer Western hypocrisy. The United States treat the Muslims with utter disdain. They bar Muslims from certain nations from entering America. They have no hesitation in bombing Muslims in Pakistan, Afghanistan, Iraq, Libya, Syria, and Yemen, killing millions of innocent Muslim civilians in the process. They incarcerate Muslims in Guantanamo Bay, and while doing all these, they now impinged on China's rights to incarcerate the rebels and terrorists in reeducation camps to learn a trade.

The simple truth is that the West has been stoking separatism in Xinjiang since the early 1950s. When the Chinese communists won in 1949, the US started to fund separatists in Tibet and Xinjiang and helped to form a movement known as the East Turkestan. The movement now, called the World Uyghur Congress, was funded by the US government through NGOs such as the National Endowment of Democracy (NED). It was the testimony of this Uyghur movement that gave birth to the false narrative that 1 million Uyghurs were detained in concentration camps. Below are some articles which depict a more accurate picture of the situation in Xinjiang and the myriad lies and propaganda perpetuated by the Western media in order to demonize China.

Reference: More materials for the above Xinjiang issues can be obtained from the following sites:

1. World Affairs (Objective, nonpartisan, and insightful)
2. *Xinjiang and Uyghurs—What You Are Not Being Told*
3. population-in-China/answer/Ridzwan-Abdul-Rahman
   https://www.quora.com/What-s-happening-with-the-Uyghur-
4. *The Black Hand – ETIM*
5. *The Uyghur Issue by* Andre Vltchek, Global Research

THE UYGHUR ISSUE

By Andre Vitchek, Global Research

"For some time, I have been warning the world that the West, and the United States in particular, are helping to radicalize the Uyghurs in Xinjiang Province and outside.

And not only that: I clearly mapped movement of the Uyghur radicals through some countries like Indonesia, towards Turkey, from where they are then injected into brutal war zones like Idlib in Syria. I worked in Idlib area, with the Syrian commanders, and I spoke at length with the Syrian internally displaced people; victims of the Uyghur genocidal attacks.

The majority of Uyghur people are Muslims. They have their own, ancient, specific culture and most of them are, of course, very decent human beings. Northwest China is their home.

The "problem" is that Urumqi, Xinjiang, are located on the main branch of BRI (The Belt and Road Initiative) – an extremely optimistic, internationalist project which is ready to connect billions of people on all continents. The BRI is infrastructural as well as cultural project, which will soon pull hundreds of millions of people out of poverty and under-development.

Washington is horrified that China is taking a lead in building a much brighter future for humanity. It is because, if

China succeeds, it could be the end of Western imperialism and neo-colonialism, leading to real freedom and independence for dozens of until now suffering nations.

Therefore, Washington has decided to act, in order to preserve the status quo and its dominance over the world.

Step one: to antagonize, provoke and to smear China by all means, be it over Hong Kong, Taiwan, South China Sea or, above mentioned "Uygur Issue".

Step two: to try to turn a part of China's constitutionally-recognized national minority – Uyghurs – into "rebels", or more precisely, terrorists.

Turkey, a member of NATO, offered the U.S. a helping hand. Uyghurs were flown with their families to Istanbul, with Turkish passports, through hubs in Southeast Asia. Then, their passports were confiscated in Istanbul. Many Uyghurs were recruited, trained, and then transported into war-torn Syria. Smaller group stayed in places like Indonesia, joining jihadi cadres there. When terrorist groups in Syria were almost thoroughly defeated, some Uyghurs were moved to Afghanistan, where I also used to work, and investigated.

Needless to say, Afghanistan has a short but important border with China.

Why all this complex operation? The answer is simple: NATO/Washington/West hope that the hardened, well-trained Uyghur jihadi fighters will eventually return home to Xinjiang. There, they would start to fight for "independence", and while doing that, they would sabotage the BRI.

This way, China would be injured, and its most powerful global project (BRI) would be disrupted.

The Chinese government is, naturally, alarmed. It is clear that the West has prepared brilliant trap: 1) If China does nothing, it will have to face extremely dangerous terrorist threat on its own territory (remember Soviet Union being dragged into Afghanistan, and mortally injured by Western trained, financed and supported Mujahedeen? West has long history of using Islam for its Machiavellian designs). 2) If China does something to protect itself, it will get attacked by the Western media and politicians. Precisely this is what is happening now.

The Opium Trade in China

Julia Lovell's *Opium War* novel succinctly described the shameful period of British-Chinese relations. Her book depicts the episode as "the original sin of Western Imperialism in East Asia that forced China to open itself to a century of humiliation, conquest, and exploitation until Chairman Mao came to sweep all that away."

In history, it was a glaring example that China was a victim of Western Imperialism and subjugation. At a severe cost of human lives that resulted in the first and second opium war, China was forced at the barrel of Western allies' guns to open up its country for the sale of opium to its Chinese citizens.

That dark period in British history will always be a grim reminder of its sordid and shameful past which unfortunately will continue to shape its relations with China till modern times. In the British Museum, they still display artifacts of a distant past when the British burned the emperor's summer palace and pillaged many of its treasures which till today refuse to surrender to its rightful owner. A brutal act of desecration of China's imperial heritage.

The First Opium War (1839–1842) was fought between the British and the Chinese and the Second Opium War (1856–1860) was the Anglo-French war between Britain and France against China. Both conflicts resulted in the victory for the foreign forces, and China ended surrendering commercial privileges and legal and territorial concessions in China.

It began an era of public humiliations denoted by the unequal treaties and resulted in the weakening of the Qing Dynasty which subsequently was toppled by the Chinese Republicans.

Modern-Day Hong Kong

The unequal treaties signed after the opium war ceded Hong Kong and five other concessionaires to Britain. It was only in 1997 that Hong Kong was finally returned to China with certain preconditions. The label of unequal treaties should have been sufficient for China to repudiate the treaties and should have demanded the return of Hong Kong without any conditions. Not only was the war fought on an evil premise of forcing a nation to consume opium, but it was a reprehensible war that was devoid of any legal right to enforce. At the first opportunity, China should have demanded the return of Hong Kong instead of waiting for the expiration period stipulated in the unequal treaty. Not only should China demand the immediate return of the territories, but also should demand payment of all compensations paid for the loss of the war which resulted in the unequal treaties. The Western countries, which instituted those punitive compensations and started the war, has no legal or moral rights to demand any compensations. China should not be pressured even to accept a theoretical state of one country, two systems. However for the sake of continuity and economic stability, perhaps China could have weighed in on the peaceful progress of the small island state.

The spark that triggered the 2019–2020 mass demonstration of Hong Kong citizens was the proposed legislation of the 2019 Hong Kong Extradition Bill. The subsequent withdrawal of the bill by the Hong Kong legislature did not seem to appease the demonstrators. However, evidence revealed that other sinister hands were involved in instigating violence to destabilize Hong Kong and a further agenda of stabilizing mainland China.

Despite the withdrawal of the extradition bill which was the cause of the initial mass demonstration, the continuation of violent demonstration, the arson of public buildings, and the use of firebombs to cause public disorder all bear the hallmarks of foreign intervention and support. The National Endowment for Democracy founded in 1983 was funded by Congress, and it has a history of political interference in other countries.

What has begun as a call to withdraw a proposed bill that would allow the extradition of legal suspects for trial in Mainland China cascaded into a wider call for universal suffrage. The irony of the demand which was not acknowledged by the protestors was that for the 150 years of colonial rule, no such universal suffrage was given to the citizens of Hong Kong. Why are they demanding universal suffrage now? The governor and all important public posts were appointed from London, and no elections for any of those posts were ever taken. The sad part is that the young protestors did not fully comprehend the full extent and the manner in which Hong Kong was administered for the last 150 years under colonial rule.

The blame should have been directed at the Ministry of Education in Hong Kong. Why was no effort been taken to educate the young generation of Hong Kong as to the historical aberration that the nation-state metamorphosed under colonial rule for 150 years? Was the young generation aware of the humiliation their fathers had to endure and the discriminatory laws that were foisted in their own land? That certain areas and parks were prohibited to the Chinese with a derogatory label prominently displayed that "Chinese and Dogs are not allowed to enter." The truth was the Chinese were treated as third-class citizens in their own land. Yet is it not ironic that this present generation of Hongkies could flagrantly exhibit their loyalty and patriotism to the US and UK by marching and displaying the star-spangled and Union Jack flags? Their forefathers would turn in the graves to witness such a foolish sense of misplaced trust in foreigners who had not long ago subjugated their older generation.

Quite rightly so, China has characterized the protest as instigated by foreign interests and viewed it as interference in their domestic affairs.

The surge in violence followed by tear gas and Molotov cocktails, chaos in transport, firebombing of subways and tunnel toll booths have resulted in the inability of businesses to operate. With no sign of any pullback of foreign interference to stabilize Hong Kong and the expectation it might have a domino effect in the mainland, the Chinese communist party at their National People's Congress move to introduce a national security law for Hong Kong. The National Security Act would "prevent, frustrate, and punish" threats to national security by outlawing acts of secession, subversion, and terrorism in Hong Kong.

During the ongoing National People's Congress session in Beijing, Chinese Foreign Minister Wang Yi assured concerns about the new law and that it would not have any effect on the city's autonomy or freedoms. According to him, the proposed legislation would only direct at a "very narrow category of acts that seriously jeopardize national security" such as "treason, secession, sedition, or subversion," he said. He further added that the law would have "no impact on Hong Kong's high degree of autonomy, the rights and freedom of Hong Kong residents, or the legitimate rights and interests of foreign investors in Hong Kong" but "instead of becoming unnecessarily worried, people should have more confidence in Hong Kong's future. This will improve Hong Kong's legal system and bring more stability, a stronger rule of law and a better business environment to Hong Kong."

A security bill was supposed to be enacted in 2003, but the bill was shelved after half a million people took to the streets to oppose the legislation, fearing it would curb their rights and freedom. Hence it was the failure of the Hong Kong legislature that led to the NPC to draft the security bill.

China would have weighed in the consequences of this action, but under the circumstance, it was the right decision. Foreign funding from the NED and interference of CIA operatives were directing some of the violent protests. The situation became dire and businesses could not function. If China had not acted with the introduction of the security law, Hong Kong would also have suffered economically with the frequent disruptions and violent rallies. China, therefore, was correct in passing the security law to reign in those guilty of fomenting the disturbance. Its sovereignty has been threatened by outside forces which had begun to instigate some of the honkies to seek independence for Hong Kong. Certainly, China cannot allow the nation-state to seek independence and perhaps become a vassal state of the US right in the front door of China. That would be unthinkable. China would rather let Hong Kong lose its shine as a financial center. Further, China has already planned for Shanghai to take over from Hong Kong. For now, China can afford to let Hong Kong slip back to its role as a fishing village with no important role to play.

The protest by two hundred parliamentarians and policymakers from twenty-three countries condemning Beijing's move as sheer hypocrisy. Hong Kong is an inalienable part of China, and as a sovereign nation, it has every right to promulgate any laws which it deemed fit. Why should other countries infringe on China's rights? They claimed that the law would have an effect on the "one country, two systems" blueprint. It's even a wonder why China should even adhere to such a blueprint.

Hong Kong was taken by the British under an illegal immoral unequal treaty of Nanking in1842. Any treaty made under its illegality is null and void. To fight a war to allow them to sell opium in China was not only a despicable act but also an illegal and immoral war. And to force China to hand over Hong Kong for 150 years over an illegal act was itself an act of tragic proportions. How ridiculous then for the British to even set conditions for the return of Hong Kong? By the law of equity, Britain should pay compensation for extracting the riches of Hong Kong for 150 years. That is an injustice of insurmountable proportion. And sheer arrogance for any of them to even criticize China for defending their territory against the onslaught of foreign forces attempting to cause unrest in the nation-state which is part of China. If the security act still does not effectively reign in those disruptions caused by foreign interference, China should immediately discard the one country, two-system polity and integrate Hong Kong as a province of China with all laws in uniformity with the mainland.

A well-written article by *South China Morning Post*'s Alex Lo best encapsulates the pros and cons of the Security Act which Beijing proposes to legislate as law in Hong Kong. For clarity, I herewith append his post which was written recently on May 24, 2020, in the *SCMP*.

More materials regarding the above issues can be obtained from the following sites:

1.
New Security Law Is a Masterstroke

Hong Kong can now be depoliticized and get back to reviving its economy and improving people's lives.

Alex Lo has been a *Post* columnist since 2012, covering major issues affecting Hong Kong and the rest of China. A journalist for twenty-five years, he has worked for various publications in Hong Kong and Toronto as a news reporter and editor. He has also lectured in journalism at the University of Hong Kong.

Published: 9:00 p.m., May 24, 2020

There is not the slightest doubt that foreign hands, especially US and Taiwan separatist elements, were involved in fueling the unrest. Some like Joshua Wong and Jimmy Lai, the media tycoon, were even consorting with US lawmakers to pass legislation against China. Because of such brazen secessionist elements, China had to introduce the Security law and protect its sovereignty.

An article by John Ross, a senior fellow at Chongyang Institute for financial studies under Renmin University and former director of economic and business policy for the mayor of London, best described the prevailing situation that pervades the Hong Kong diaspora.

HONG KONG SECURITY LAW

The National People's Congress on June 20, 2020, passed the Hong Kong Security Law. On June 2, Washington passed the Autonomy Act which could affect the operations of financial institutions in Hong Kong. This act came closely on the heels of another act, the Hong Kong Human Rights and Democracy Act which seeks to apply sanctions for individuals and companies that "materially contributed" to China's failure to comply with the 1984 Sino-British Joint Declaration. Quite rightly, both acts received an angry response from China. A neutral observer could see that the US Senate was clearly interfering in the internal affairs of Hong Kong, which territorially was part of China and that the latter reserved the right of exercising sovereignty over Hong Kong by passing any law it deemed fit to protect its sovereignty.

Clearly, US action was in clear violation of United Nations rule that no nation should interfere in the internal affairs of another nation, and this principle was well established in Nicaragua's case. The sheer hypocrisy of it all was their angry response of Russian interference in Donald Trump's election victory in 2016. It would be poetic justice if China's People Congress should similarly pass a law condemning the US for human rights violations against its black Americans and to invoke sanctions on its lawmakers responsible for many of the indiscriminate killings of the Black minority. Surely, if the US can pass its own laws to sanction another country, what's wrong for another country to do likewise for US violations of interference in another country? Perhaps one should ask the US and those Western countries who voice objections to those security laws whether their own country has any of those laws. There is little doubt that provocative acts of secession, terrorism, call for independence, and collusion with foreign powers are all acts against the country and are criminalized in all Western countries. So what curtailment of freedom are these Western powers screaming for as a result of the Security Law? Or are the Western powers mourning the loss of freedom to commit those treasonable acts?

Such hypocritical acts by the Western powers only further confirm their consistent display of demonizing China for anything that China does. Before continuing with such uncivilized behavior, these Western powers should reflect on their historical roles of bullying, looting, and killing civilians of small nations. They should not pretend to be the protectors of human rights and freedom when their own past is filled with atrocities that were so gross and inhuman.

By providing sanctuary and citizenships for Hongkongers who wanted to leave was tantamount to interference of Hong Kong's sovereignty. But China should not be concerned with these Western provocations but instead welcome the departure of these dissidents who are nothing but traitors and troublemakers. In fact, China should assist and facilitate their departure. If these people can betray their own country, what more their adoptive country? China would be better off getting rid of this menace festering in Hong Kong. Their departure should be a welcome relief for China.

More reference materials for the above issues can be obtained from the following links and sites:

1. **Why is the West so against the introduction of national security law in Hong Kong?**

2. **If Hong Kong had enacted national security laws on its own, Beijing wouldn't be stepping in.**

Beijing trusted Hong Kong to implement Article 23, but its trust was misplaced. The Basic Law is a two-way street—it isn't fair to accuse the central government of failing to comply with the mini-constitution when Hong Kong itself has not fulfilled its obligations.

Grenville Cross
Published: 6:30 a.m., May 29, 2020

3. **"No blue ribbons and dogs": the democracy movement has gone to the dogs.**

Published: March 16, 2020

While the culprits see violence as a means of advancing their political agenda, the Legislative Council, riven by strife, is unable to enact the laws that are necessary to protect Hong Kong.

4. **Distrust of China has blinded Hong Kong to perceive a need for national security law.**

Published: May 27, 2020
Grenville Cross SC is a criminal justice analyst.

Grenville Cross SC is a criminal justice analyst, a barrister (Queen's counsel and senior counsel), and vice chairman of the Senate of the International Association of Prosecutors. He is sentencing editor of Hong Kong Cases and Archbold Hong

Kong, and coauthor of Sentencing in Hong Kong. He was the director of public prosecutions from 1997 to 2009.

5. Hong Kong/Politics

Hong Kong slams US' Autonomy Act, urges Washington to refrain from measures that could affect financial institution operations.

Any sanctions imposed under the act "will not create an obligation for financial institutions under Hong Kong law," the spokesman says.

Published: 10:30 p.m., June 26, 2020

The US Senate on Thursday unanimously passed legislation that would impose mandatory sanctions on individuals and companies.

6. US Senate passes a bill that would punish China for Hong Kong national security law.

Published: June 30, 2020

"Any 'sanctions' imposed under the act will not create an obligation for financial institutions under Hong Kong law," the spokesman said. "We, however, urge the US side to act responsibly by refraining from taking measures that may potentially affect the normal operations of financial institutions and the vast number of customers they serve."

The US House of Representatives must now pass its own version of the bill before it can become law.

7. Explainer: How will Beijing introduce Hong Kong's national security law and who will be consulted?

Published: June 23, 2020

ANGELO GIULIANO
Published: Wednesday, November 4, 10:25 a.m.

8. *The "White" World Against The "Non-White"*

The Divide of the World regarding the Hong Kong National Security Law.

The West has all along been racist, today is no different.

Hong Kong has suffered a year of rioting, lootings, and lynching of innocent citizens, terrorism. For China, it was time to act.

China has taken the decision to enact a National Security Law on Hong Kong that was long overdue. We have been waiting twenty-three years, there was a huge support of 3 million signatures petition which the Western Mass Media has completely occulted in its reports.

The riots and unrest were sponsored by the USA through NGOs, local tycoons, and the DDP party of Taiwan.

Recently at the UN Human Rights Council, there was a vote in support and against the Hong Kong National Security Law.

The divide has many interesting points to teach us.

Twenty-seven countries condemning China:

Australia, Austria, Belgium, Belize, Canada, Denmark, Estonia, Finland, France, Iceland, Ireland, Germany, Japan, Latvia, Liechtenstein, Lithuania, Luxembourg, Marshall Islands, Netherlands, New Zealand, Norway, Palau, Slovakia, Slovenia, Sweden, Switzerland, and the UK.

Fifty-three countries that backed up China:

China, Antigua and Barbuda, Bahrain, Belarus, Burundi, Cambodia, Cameroon, Central African Republic, Comoros, Congo-Brazzaville, Cuba, Djibouti, Dominica, Egypt, Equatorial Guinea, Eritrea, Gabon, Gambia, Guinea, Guinea-Bissau, Iran, Iraq, Kuwait, Laos, Lebanon, Lesotho, Mauritania, Morocco, Mozambique, Myanmar, Nepal, Nicaragua, Niger, North Korea, Oman, Pakistan, Palestine, Papua New Guinea, Saudi Arabia, Sierra Leone, Somalia, South Sudan, Sri Lanka, Sudan, Suriname, Syria, Tajikistan, Togo, UAE, Venezuela, Yemen, Zambia, and Zimbabwe.

The contrast is most obvious.

The countries condemning China:

- They are all "white" countries except Japan, which is still under occupation since WW2, not a complete sovereign state and a lapdog of the US.
- The USA is not on the list because it left the Human Rights Council.
- Belgium, France, UK, Japan, Germany: ex empires and colonizers.
- Canada, Australia, Germany, New Zealand: genocide past (Indians, Jews, Maoris).
- Most of those countries are NATO members (or friends).
- All are "rich" countries.
- They are "self-proclaimed" members of the liberal democratic and "free" world.

While on the other side, in the supporters of China, we have:

- Not a single white country.
- Most are poor countries.

- Most have been colonized in the past.
- Most have signed the Belt and Road Initiative.
- Most are under pressure to adopt a "Western-style democracy."

We can clearly see the divide between the "white" world against the "non-white" world.

- The "haves" ($) versus the "have-nots" ($): rich and poor divide.
- The aggressors versus the victims of aggression.

There is so much hypocrisy coming from the "white" world. Hong Kong is just a "pawn" in the imperialistic agenda of the white world to put a stop to the reemergence of China.

Here it is important to look at the big picture.

China is leading a world that had been colonized. It is about the oppressed versus the aggressor white-world that wants to keep the rest of the world enslaved through the dollar hegemony and under military threat.

This has nothing to do with freedom, democracy, human rights, or the future of Hong Kong. Only China cares about Hong Kong and its people.

The West was always racist and still is. They can support the BLM movement at home while keeping its racist and imperialistic agenda.

It is about time people start to wake up and denounce this hypocrisy.

The "China and Russia" block is the only hope for most of the oppressed world to regain its human dignity, for a better share of wealth, more equality, and peace.

The future will be multipolar, I hope. The fight starts in Hong Kong, and there will be other challenges ahead—Taiwan, Venezuela, Iran.

All will be used in the China–USA proxy war.

Angelo Giuliano
Published: July 3, 2020

9. US Senate passes a bill that could punish China for Hong Kong national security law.

Proposed congressional actions involving Hong Kong are "more symbolic than substantive," an analyst says.

The measure now goes to the House of Representatives for debate on its own version of the legislation.

Published: 12:35 a.m., June 26, 2020

Why you can trust SCMP
4.4k

10. Senator Chris Van Hollen, a Democrat from Maryland, introduced the Hong Kong Autonomy Act.

Photo: Amanda Andrade-Rhoades/Bloomberg.

The US Senate approved legislation on Thursday that would strengthen the US government's ability to sanction those violating China's commitments to Hong Kong under the Sino-British Joint Declaration and the Basic Law.

01:08

11. **US Senate passes a bill that could punish China for Hong Kong national security law.**

01:56

12. **Hong Kong is no longer autonomous from China, US determines.**

Hong Kong Democracy Council's Samuel Chu, who has been involved in drumming up support for the bill on Capitol Hill, said it was most likely that the legislation would be ultimately moved as part of the annual National Defence Authorisation Act rather than as a stand-alone bill, given the shrinking amount of time left on the congressional calendar as election season looms.

02:06

13. **US President Donald Trump signs Hong Kong human rights bills into law.**

14. **The US imposes visa restrictions on Chinese officials over Hong Kong national security law.**

Secretary of State Mike Pompeo does not identify any individuals who will be targeted by the new sanctions.

Move by the State Department comes a day after the US Senate passed the Hong Kong Autonomy Act.

Published: 12:27 a.m., June 27, 2020

Why you can trust SCMP
4.2k

15. US Secretary of State Mike Pompeo announced the new visa restrictions.

Photo: AP

The US State Department has imposed its first wave of visa restrictions against Chinese officials in retaliation for Beijing's policies in Hong Kong, Secretary of State Mike Pompeo announced on Friday.

01:56

16. Hong Kong is no longer autonomous from China, US determines.

Friday's announcement follows the State Department's determination last month, in a report mandated by the Hong Kong Policy Act of 1992 and the Hong Kong Human Rights & Democracy Act of 2019, that the city no longer warrants different treatment from mainland China.

The sanction announcement was the latest sign of just how far the US–China relationship has fallen amid a trade war, a pandemic, and generally soaring distrust between Washington and Beijing.

01:38

17. The US designates four more Chinese media organizations as "state propaganda outlets."

US designates four more Chinese media organizations as "state propaganda outlets"

China's embassy in Washington pushed back, arguing that China's Constitution and Hong Kong's Basic Law supersede any authority the Sino-British Joint Declaration may have had because "all rights and obligations of the British side as prescribed in the Joint Declaration were completed" when sovereignty over the city was transferred to China in 1997.

18. Hong Kong and other disagreements dominate the US– China Hawaii meeting.

Published: June 18, 2020

That pledge was reiterated last week when Pompeo and Chinese state councilor Yang Jiechi met in Hawaii to discuss a number of issues between the two countries, including Hong Kong's autonomy.

Jacob Fromer has reported from Beijing and Washington. He has a master's degree from the Fletcher School of Law and Diplomacy.

Robert Delaney is the *Post*'s North America bureau chief. He spent eleven years in China as a language student and correspondent for *Dow Jones Newswires* and *Bloomberg* and continued covering the country as a correspondent and an academic after leaving. His debut novel, *The Wounded Muse*, draws on actual events that played out in Beijing while he lived there.

INDIA VS. CHINA

The recent clash between China and India at the Ladakh region of the contested border known as the Line of Actual Control (LAC) saw the death of twenty Indian soldiers and unreported injuries and death on the Chinese side. The clashes erupted in the Himalayas over infrastructure construction. Since the China–India border friction which first ended in a brief war in 1962, such skirmishes are part of a long line that dated back decades.

In the geopolitical war with China, the US has chosen India to be its henchman, whereas traditional allies like Japan, South Korea, the Philippines, Thailand, and Malaysia have all refrain from joining any coalition with the US.

It will be a fatal mistake for India to be a US pawn in the Indo-Pacific region. The smarter playbook would be to remain friends with the US while using China to create a better understanding with Pakistan and within this period to concentrate on growth, trade, and peace.

A smarter strategy for India is to adopt China's Belt and Road Initiative which at last count had already attracted 170 countries including European nations. With good relations with China and Pakistan, India could source cheap oil and gas from

Central Asia using pipelines through Pakistan. This inevitably would solve India's future energy problem.

Economically, India should persuade China to move some of its manufacturing to India especially in the areas of electric cars and buses which will reduce pollution. India could also encourage China to invest in housing for its impoverished slums and to build infrastructure projects like the high-speed rail.

In short, India's interest would better be served if it seeks to focus on improving its economy, housing, infrastructure, healthcare, education, environment, and technological innovation rather than waste its time on being a pawn to serve US geopolitical interests. It should refrain from being led into a disastrous war by US prodding and instigation.

In 1954, Prime Minister of India Nehru went to Beijing and spent three days with Mao. During this period, both came up with the "Five Principles of Peaceful Coexistence." This resulted in the famous words, "Hindi Chini Bhai Bhai," meaning "Indians and Chinese are brothers." Hopefully, this brotherly diplomacy nurtured by Nehru will continue by Mod.

Search for:

THE EURASIA TIMES

EXPERT REVIEWS: 2 days ago
Why China's Belligerent 'Five Finger' Strategy Is a 'Herculean Challenge' for India & Its Army?

FEATURED 1 week ago
Four Times Faster Than US' Tomahawks, Why Indian BrahMos Missiles Pose a Grave Risk to China?

ASIA PACIFIC 1 week ago
Chinese J-11 Fighter Jets Conduct Large-Scale War Drills Near Indian Border – WATCH

ASIA PACIFIC 3 days ago
Watch: Indian Soldiers Froze to Death in Ladakh With Their Camp Buried in Snow – Chinese Media Claims

India Buying French A-330 Airbus Refuelers Is Simply Bad Economics: Indian Military Expert

FEATURED 1 week ago
Indian Aircraft Carrier Vikrant Gears Up for Commissioning as Rafales Compete Against F-18s as Its 'Flying Machines'

Politics
Is the US behind India's "anti-China games"? Russia thinks so.

- Foreign Minister Sergey Lavrov's warning that New Delhi is being manipulated by the West in its relations with China sparks resistance
- Moscow is worried that closer New Delhi–Washington ties could affect purchases of Russian weaponry, experts say

Published: 8:00 p.m., December 14, 2020

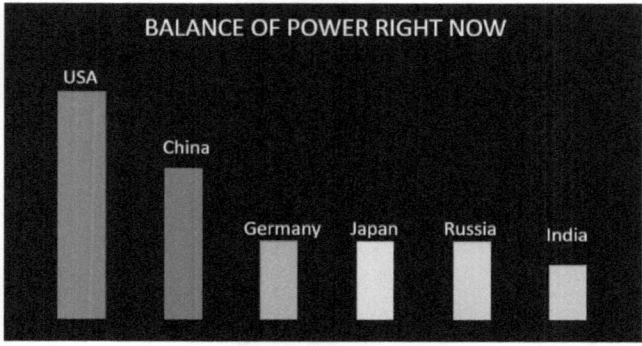

In purchasing power, China <u>surpassed </u>the US in 2014. And as I show in my blog post, China will very likely be the largest economy by nominal GDP within five years (by 2025) as well.

QUAD ALLIANCE

India invited Australia to participate in the Exercise Malabar 2020 in the Bay of Bengal toward the end of this year. The other participants in the Malabar Exercise are Japan, Australia, and the US. The US formally established the QUAD (Quadrilateral Security Dialogue) Alliance with the purpose of emulating the "NATO" Alliance except this was called the "Asian NATO."

The purpose of US forming this alliance is to contain China by using the three countries to form a pressure bloc against China. However, with the exception of Australia, India and Japan have different motives for engaging in the alliance. India's vested interest in the alliance was its territorial dispute with China in the Ladakh region. Japan's interest in China was the Senkaku (Diayou) islands. Both have different reasons for being in the bloc.

Australia is the odd man out. It is in the Quad Alliance merely at the behest of the US. It has no land or territory dispute with China. The only reason it is in Quad is because the US wishes Australia to sow discord with China. And for their foolishness, they have suffered economically. The Quad Alliance will pose no threat to China's interest. China does not pose any threats in the Indian ocean and instead both countries should strive for cooperation in areas of common interest. In the final analysis, India cannot expect the US to be dragged into any military conflict with China in the Ladakh region.

Both India and Japan joined the Quad Alliance because of their own vested interests (India because of its Ladakh region dispute with China, and Japan because of the Senkaku island dispute). Australia's geographical area is not being threatened by China's Southeast Asia Nine-Dash Line claim, and they joined the Quad Alliance merely to show their support of the US as members of the Five Eyes Alliance.

Australia's inconsistent foreign policy will seriously impact their economy when China uses its trading leverage to punish Australia for its hostile attitude toward them. By being a lapdog of the US, it has provoked a retaliation from China which has started to ban the imports of beef, barley, wine, cotton, and iron ore, a trade value at $135 billion in 2019.

The China–India Border Dispute: Its Origins and Impact

For the first time in decades, soldiers stationed along a remote front line between the two countries engaged in deadly hand-to-hand combat.

Leaders have sought to settle the conflict as it ripples out into the economy and wider international relations.

SCMP Reporters

Published: 10:00 a.m., July 29, 2020

Why you can trust SCMP
180

An Indian Air Force aircraft flies near Leh, in Ladakh, on June 27. (Photo: AFP)

In mid-June 2020, in a remote Himalayan valley, Chinese and Indian troops faced each other, armed only with sticks and rocks. By the time the confrontation in the Galwan Valley was over, at least twenty Indian soldiers were dead, and seventy-six were wounded. The casualties on the Chinese side are not known.

What happened in the Galwan Valley?

The clashes took place at more than 4,000 meters (14,000 feet) above sea level in an area between Indian-controlled Ladakh and Chinese-controlled Aksai Chin on June 15, but exactly what caused it is not clear. The deadly confrontation came after another clash on May 5, and during an attempt by both sides to deescalate the subsequent six-week standoff.

The troops did not have guns because of a 1996 agreement the two sides signed to build trust and begin to settle the border issue. Instead, the soldiers fought with fists, sticks, and rocks.

An Indian colonel and two Indian soldiers were reportedly killed in the combat, while seventeen others died overnight from their wounds.

The condition of the wounded was worsened by the lack of oxygen and the sub-zero temperatures. Search and rescue efforts were hampered by the rough terrain.

China has yet to clarify the cause of the conflict or how many casualties it sustained, saying only that its forces had "light injuries."

01:59
Death toll rises to 20 in border clash between India and China

When did the border trouble begin?

The dispute dates back at least to the Simla Convention in 1914, when representatives of British India and Tibet agreed to a de facto eastern border known as the McMahon Line. Beijing never agreed to the line, but the Indian government has adopted the boundary as the effective border in the area between India and China.

In 1962, India lost a four-week war with China, with People's Liberation Army troops crossing the McMahon Line in the east and advancing in the west. India claimed that China grabbed some 43,000 sq km in Ladakh/Aksai Chin, an area roughly the size of Switzerland.

The two sides could not agree on an official border, so they reached a temporary truce along an unofficial border in the west known as the Line of Actual Control. But they have never agreed on where the line is. Conflicts continued as the Chinese and Indian armies accuse each other of breaches, reaching a peak in 1967, when there were hundreds of casualties.

The LAC is also sometimes used loosely to refer to the entire disputed border between the two countries.

THE EURASIA TIMES

Russia Slams the QUAD; Puts India in the Firing Line as Moscow Inches Closer to China
C. Uday Bhaskar

How Indo-Pacific tensions reflect a post-coronavirus new world order of conflict and contradiction

- The emerging global order of 2021 and beyond will be more of a "contra-polar" world, where contradictory policy pursuits and contrarian impulses are the norm.
- China's ability to avoid becoming the glue that provides cohesion to the US–India partnership will shape the contours of the next decade's geopolitics.

With new export controls, the US takes another step to clamp down on China

New US rules restricting exports to China to prevent sensitive technologies from the use by military seen to worsen relations.

"This is just one rule out of a number of actions we've seen that are impacting China. And there is more to come," legal expert says.

Why you can trust SCMP
623

US President Donald Trump's campaign to limit exports of sensitive technologies to China has accelerated in recent months. (Photo: AFP)

New US rules restricting exports to China to prevent sensitive technologies from being used by the Chinese military are the latest development in the deteriorating relationship between the two countries. And the worst is yet to come, legal experts say.

CHINA AND PAKISTAN

Pakistan was the third non-communist country and the first Muslim country to establish formal diplomatic relations with China on May 21, 1951. In 1963 the two countries concluded a border agreement through peaceful negotiations. During this time, China was isolated and Pakistan provided China with a window to interact with the outside world. In 1970, Pakistan facilitated the visit of US President Nixon to China which resulted in the first-ever official contact between the US and China. This subsequently led to the normalization of Sino-American relations.

In 1989 during the Tiananmen protest, Pakistan and Cuba were the only two countries which gave support to China. On geopolitical issues, China supports Pakistan stance on Kashmir and Pakistan supports China on Tibet, Xinjiang, and Taiwan.

China and Pakistan have established strong military ties. And both countries have several joint projects for military equipment, ammunition, and technological assistance. In addition to ventures in aircraft and military equipment investments, China has also invested in Pakistan's Gwadar deep-sea port which is strategically at the entrance of the Straits of Hormuz.

In the world stage, at the United Nations on July 19, 2019, Pakistan was one of fifty countries that supported China's policies in Xinjiang. And in November 2019, Pakistan was one of fifty-four countries that signed a joint statement supporting China's policies in Xinjiang.

Then in June 2020, Pakistan again was one of fifty-three countries that supported Hong Kong Security Law at the United Nations.

The proposed China–Pakistan Economic Corridor (CPEC) will connect China and Pakistan through the Central Asian countries with a highway connecting Kashgar to Khunjerab to Gwadar. From this deep-sea port of Gwadar, oil from the Persian Gulf can economically be transported by land to China instead of sailing to the port in Shanghai some 16,000 kilometers away. At the moment, 60 percent of Persian Gulf oil is transported by ship and the shipment takes a couple of months being exposed to pirates, weather, and political risks. Using Gwadar Port, the distance and cost of transportation could be reduced considerably.

China and Pakistan have nurtured a close and strategic partnership that will benefit both nations, one which has already endured the test of time.

Reference material can be read from the following sites.

China–Pakistan: A Journey of Friendship (1950–2020)
By Zamir Ahmed Awan
Source: *Global Times*
Published: 11:55:52, May 21, 2020

After Morocco, Pakistan Likely to Accept Israel with Some Pre-Conditions: Expert Analysis

Beyond Ideologies: The Many Tehreeks of Pakistan
By Niha Dagia
December 1, 2020

By offering condolences for Khadim Hussain Rizvi's death, is the TTP planning to expand its influence into the political realm?

CHINA AND PHILIPPINES

Relations between China and the Philippines for a long time have been warm and cordial. The Filipino–Chinese constitute one of the largest overseas Chinese communities in Southeast Asia. The Filipino–Chinese have assimilated very well economically and politically and are well represented in all levels of Philippine society.

However, of late, both countries have faced a surge in tension brought about by territorial disputes in the West Philippine Seas. The territorial dispute in April 2012 which escalated over the Scarborough Shoal was the result of Chinese illegal occupation, illegal construction of infrastructure, and encroachment within the Philippines exclusive economic zone (EEZ). Bilateral ties were strained when in January 2013, the Philippine government filed an arbitration case against China under the United National Convention on the Law of the Sea (UNCLOS) challenging the legality of the claim of the nine-dash line. Although the subsequent decision was in favor of the Philippine government, China did not recognize the ruling.

Despite tension caused by territorial disputes, China and the Philippines should focus on bilateral issues that would benefit both countries. The Philippines must deal diplomatically with China to settle territorial disputes despite divergent geopolitical and security issues. And China should treat the Philippines with respect and try to resolve territorial disputes in accordance with existing maritime law. China must display fairness in its claim and must respect the territorial sovereignty of the Philippines in accordance with existing maritime laws. China would gain respect from other states in the region if such territorial disputes can be settled amicably without the involvement of any third party.

Reference: reader can read materials relating to the Philippines by accessing the website below.

Philippine Standard Time:
Sunday, December 6, 2020, 10:47:28 p.m.

Philippines–China Relations: Beyond the Territorial Disputes

China Refuses to Quit on the Philippines

China may have missed a golden opportunity to see the VFA end, but Beijing is still determined to exploit gaps between the US and its ally.

By Derek Grossman
https://www.scmp.com/week-asia/politics/article/3113101/trumps-parting-gift-philippines-us29-million-defence-equipment

Donald Trump's parting gift to Philippines: Defence equipment worth US$29 million

- The offering from US Acting Defence Secretary Christopher Miller was the latest gift to Manila from Washington as it aims to counter China in the region.

- An article written by Miller for a local newspaper rejecting China's claims in the South China Sea drew a harsh rebuke from Beijing's envoy to Manila.

Why you can trust SCMP

CHINA AND VIETNAM

China and Vietnam share a common border stretching over 1,281 kilometers. The relations between these two socialist countries have lately been hostile. Although China supported North Vietnam during the war with the US in the Vietnam War, their relations have been soured after their reunification in 1975 and both fought a war from 1979 to 1990.

China and Vietnam's dispute has always centered around territorial issues from the lack of delineation of Vietnam's territorial waters in the Gulf of Tonkin and the claim of sovereignty over the Spratly and Paracel Islands in the South China Sea. The potential discovery of oil in the Gulf of Tonkin increased tensions between China and Vietnam. In the 1950s, China controlled the Paracel Islands and the rest by Vietnam. After the reunification of South and North Vietnam in 1975, Vietnam took control of the South Vietnam-controlled Spratly Island and cancelled its earlier renunciation of its claim of the Paracel Islands.

Not to aggravate relations with China, Vietnam has so far resisted filing a case with the United Nations. Instead, it has sought to engage China using four components of "Internationalizing the disputes," resorting to "multilateralism framework" (via ASEAN), deterring any military conflict with China and keeping channels open for negotiations.

So far China has not been conciliatory in seeking some form of settlement with respect to the territorial disputes. Vietnam's attempt to internationalize the South China disputes have only received sporadic support in view of the pandemic affecting most countries.

China should try to settle territorial disputes with Vietnam to avoid pushing Vietnam into the US orbit. The US is now galvanizing a front consisting of Southeast Asian countries to confront and contain China's aggressiveness. So far almost all countries in the region with the exception of Japan, India, and Australia have remained neutral. But will such neutrality continue when most of the countries also have similar territorial disputes under China's nine-dash claim? There is no legal basis for China to continue with its nine-dash claim, and a lot of goodwill could be obtained by China if it stops claiming territories and the South China Sea using the nine-dash historical claim.

China and Vietnam share a lengthy border and with peaceful cooperation between the two countries, a lot of positive development could be achieved. China does not need a neighbor that is friendly to the US that will only create another front that is hostile to China.

It is in China's interest to have a friendly neighbor on their side rather than an enemy that is friendly toward the US. Strategically, it does not make sense for China to have Vietnam as an enemy. Territorial disputes in the Gulf of Tonkin can easily be resolved if both parties make concessions. No point for China to fight over the Paracel and Spratly Islands when there are so many other important issues at stake. A friendly Vietnam could open up an economic corridor for China to further extend their BRI into the country proper. There will be vast opportunities for both countries to develop infrastructure, agriculture, and technological development in so many fields. It will also provide an instant market for China's products and goods and better cooperation could accelerate two-way trade that will benefit both economies.

China has to reevaluate its strategy in the South China Sea. It cannot afford to make enemies with so many countries in the Southeast Asia region with their nine-dash claim. It is a behemoth power in this region and China has to cultivate friends and earn their respect. It cannot project its image using brute force to handle territorial disputes under the historical claim of the nine-dash line which contravenes international maritime laws. Only with a peaceful and amicable settlement among all vested parties in the territorial dispute can we see prosperity in this region. Not otherwise.

Reference: Materials relating to Vietnam can also be obtained from the site listed below.

DECEMBER 4, 2020, LAST UPDATED 15:58 ET

Vietnam, Under Increasing Pressure from China, Mulls a Shift into America's Orbit

The US and Vietnam have already built close strategic ties, and Pentagon officials regard Hanoi as one of America's most important emerging military partners.

https://carnegieendowment.org/2020/09/30/rough-waters-ahead-for-vietnam-china-relations-pub-82826

Joshua Kurlantzick
Thursday, January 30, 2020

THE DIPLOMAT

Vietnam Is Losing Its Best Friends to China

Over the past few years, China's economic gravity has begun to pull Cambodia and Laos out of Vietnam's orbit.

Rough Waters Ahead for Vietnam-China Relations

By Huong Le Thu
September 30, 2020

East Asia Pacific
China, Vietnam Try to Make Amends After Stormy Start to 2020

By Ralph Jennings
September 02, 2020, 10:41 a.m.

CHINA AND THAILAND

China and Thailand's bilateral relations are principally dominated by trade. Thailand's recognition and support of One-China policy have enabled the country to gain access to capital and the huge Chinese mainland market.

After the coup in 2014, relations improved further, and a private Chinese company was given the contract to build a high-speed rail megaproject connecting Bangkok with Nong Khai in northern Thailand. And the Chinese were allowed to build dams in the Mekong.

China's transformation into a global economic powerhouse in the twenty-first century has led to an increase in foreign investments in the Thai economy. China is Thailand's largest export market and is the largest importer of China's goods.

Under Prime Minister Prayuth Chan-Ocha, Thailand ordered main battle tanks and submarines costing more than US$1 billion. Thailand entered into an agreement with China to build a joint commercial arms factory in Khon Kaen where it will assemble, produce, and maintenance of land weapon system for the Thai army.

Under the current Thai administration, relations with China have improved considerably. Since the 2014 coup, Thailand has become the leading trading partner of China and its largest source of foreign investments.

Thailand's cozy relations with China has put a strain on US–Thai relations, and it expects the situation to deteriorate even further. It appears Thailand's participation in the Belt and Road Initiative has cemented relations with China, and with several investments ongoing and on the card, US presence will gradually diminish in importance.

Reference: More reading can be obtained from the site below.

THE DIPLOMAT

New US Envoy to Thailand Walks Tightrope Amid Alliance Strain

US–Thai relations have entered a new tumultuous phase.
By Shawn W. Crispin

US–Thailand Relations on a Razor's Edge

Further delays in polls could lead to a more punitive US response.
By Shawn W. Crispin
August 11, 2015

Thai Junta Chief Slams US Policy
The US needs a better "tailor," the General says.
By Prashanth Parameswaran
March 18, 2015
National security.

America Should Be Realistic About Its Alliance with Thailand
By Zachary Abuza
January 2, 2020

CHINA AND MALAYSIA

Malaysia has been the largest trading partner with China among all the ASEAN countries. It ranks third in Asia after Japan and Korea. It is the major investor in infrastructure especially in the construction of a railroad called the East Coast Rail Link from the west to the east coast (ECRL), a key BRI project for China. In 2014, Najib, the Prime Minister then, pledged to increase bilateral trade and agreed to upgrade economic and financial cooperation. China's economic transformation in the last century has led to an increase in investments in Malaysia and the other ASEAN countries.

Sadly, China and Malaysia's relation has not been without any tensions and conflicts. As with the other ASEAN countries, Malaysia's disputes have been predominantly on territorial issues brought on by China's historical nine-dash claim. Two contentious issues that brought about tensions was the illegal fishing by Chinese fishing vessels at the Luconia shoal and the constant harassment of Malaysian energy exploration ship. However, Malaysia has chosen "quiet diplomacy" in dealing with China's historical maritime claims. Despite several overtures for Malaysia to take the US side in confronting China on the South China Sea claims, Malaysia has been adamant that it would not be dragged into geopolitical issues between the two superpowers. It prefers to remain neutral and to resolve their territorial issues with China on a bilateral basis between the two countries.

Malaysia attached importance in its bilateral trade with China and determine to use diplomacy to settle its territorial disputes with China.

As an important power in the Southeast Asia Region, China should exercise diplomacy and restraint in resolving each and every territorial dispute it has with all ASEAN countries. Obviously, in the long term, it would be to China's advantage that he shows magnanimity by settling with all the Southeast Asian countries individually and amicably. The last thing China wants is to have a confrontation with these countries that could all flock to the US side to form a bloc to air their grievances. Even by making concessions on the territorial issues, China could gain many friends with increase trade, investments, and goodwill among all the Southeast Asian countries.

Reference: Materials relating to the above article can be obtained from the following sites.

Malaysia Has Strong Relations with China, Not 'Pawn' in Big Powers Rivalry: Ambassador

By Xie Wenting and Bai Yunyi
Source: *Global Times*
Published: October 12, 2020, 18:46:11

THE DIPLOMAT

China-Malaysia Relations
Malaysia in China's Belt and Road
By Mercy A. Kuo

Insights from Chow Bing Ngeow
November 23, 2020

Malaysia–China Relations in the Time of COVID-19
Author: Johan Saravanamuttu, RSIS
April 1, 2020

China, Malaysia Reach Wide Range of Consensuses on Cooperation: Wang Yi
Source: Xinhua
Editor: Huaxia
October 14, 2020, 00:50:28

Malaysia Rebukes Beijing as South China Sea 'Lawfare' Heats Up
July 31, 2020

"If we give in to the narratives and pressure of big powers, there is potential for Asean countries to align themselves with certain high-placed countries," Hishammuddin said.

Leaders from the Asia-Pacific Economic Cooperation (APEC) grouping.

The report did not mention the sea row but said, "the two sides also had an in-depth exchange of views on jointly coping with the current unstable and uncertain international situation."

John Power
Published: 9:30 p.m., August 5, 2020

CHINA AND SOUTH KOREA

South Korea is in a unique situation where it is reliant on China for its economic survival and reliant on the US for its country's security. South Korea's economy has been running a trade surplus with China which hit a record of US$ 32 billion in 2009 and total trade surpassed US$ 300 billion in 2014.

But unlike India and Japan, South Korea does not have any territorial dispute with China. That's why it is not in the Quad Alliance with India, Japan, Australia, and the US. Nevertheless there are few occasions when the two countries does experienced tensions in their relations. In 2016, Chinese fishing boats rammed and sunk a South Korean coast guard vessel. This happened when South Korean coast guards were trying to stop forty Chinese fishing boats from illegal fishing off South Korea's west coast.

Another incident which created tensions between South Korea and China was the deployment of Terminal High-Altitude Area Defence (THAAD) which was in response to the nuclear and missile threats by North Korea. The US explanation was that the missiles was only a purely defensive measure aimed at North Korea and did not threaten China's security interest. Naturally China opposed the deployment of the THAAD missiles as it was concerned that it was a measure to contain China.

Despite China's objection, South Korea deployed THAAD in 2017. China did not apply any sanctions measures but allowed its citizens to protest. China's citizens boycotted Korean cars like Hyundai, and Korean products were removed from supermarket shelves and travel companies and tourists were discouraged to travel to South Korea.

The boycott measures by China severely affected South Korea's economy which placed heavy reliance on China's exports and imports. It was only a year later that things managed to return to normalcy.

South Korea has to do a delicate balancing act to placate the two superpowers that were involved in geopolitical issues. On the one hand, it has to soothe US effort to contain China and on the other hand it has to avoid causing tensions with its giant neighbor which may resort to applying economic sanctions on them.

China can help to resolve the South Korean dilemma of a belligerent North Korea by reigning in the latter's hostility toward the South. A peaceful settlement of the two Koreas should ease tensions in the peninsula and perhaps should dispense with any need for the South to have any security alliance with the US. Once the North does not pose any threats to the South, there is no further need for the US to station their troops in South Korea. It is in China's security interest in the long term if US bases are permanently removed from the Korean Peninsula. And the way this can be done only if South Korea is assured of their own security and that a North Korean threat and hostility no longer exist.

Reference materials can be read from the following sites.

TRANS-PACIFIC VIEW

Is the US-South Korea Alliance in Trouble?
Recent trends suggest that US–South Korea relations are increasingly strained.
By Patrick Monaghan
April 21, 2018

China-South Korea Relations: A Delicate Détente
By Kristian McGuire
The thaw in relations is not going to last long.
February 27, 2018

South Korea and China Make Amends. What Now?
By Clint Work
Shortly after Trump came to South Korea, President Moon met with China's top leaders, solidifying a thaw in relations.
November 18, 2017

South Korea Stops THAAD: Strategic Misstep?
By Mercy A. Kuo
Insights from Soo Kim.
June 22, 2017

CHINA AND JAPAN

Historically, China and Japan have a long history of animosity which ended in two wars fought between the two nations. The First Sino-Japanese War fought in 1894–1895 was during the rule of the Qing Dynasty. The Qing Dynasty was defeated, and by the Treaty of Shimonoseki, Korea became fully independent, and Taiwan was ceded to Japan. In addition, Japan also annexed the Diaoyudao/Senkaku Islands in late 1895.

The Second Sino-Japanese War was fought between the Republic of China and Japanese empire from 1937 to 1945. The war was the result of long-term Japanese Imperialist policies to expand its political and military influence and to secure access to raw materials, food, and labor. China was no match for the Japanese modernized army and lost its major cities of Beijing, Shanghai, and the capital city of Nanjing in 1937 (which resulted in the Rape of Nanjing). In 1941, Japan launched an attack on Pearl Harbor and declared war on the United States.

The war ended when the US dropped two hydrogen bombs in Nagasaki and Hiroshima, and Japan formally surrendered on September 2, 1945. The aftermath of the war saw the return of all Chinese territories with the exception of Taiwan which was given to the Nationalist Party under Chiang Kai Shek, and the

Diaoyudao/Senkaku Islands which was retained under Japan rule and Vladivostok still under Russian rule.

Perhaps one should question the motives of those key powers why all those territories unlawfully taken by Japan during World War II was never returned to its rightful owner thus creating a situation of territorial dispute between the various countries. Japan annexed the Diaoyudao/Senkaku Island under the Treaty of Shimonoseki in 1895; Taiwan was similarly annexed under the same treaty and given to the Nationalist Party under Chiang Kai Shek. Under the Treaty of Aigun signed in 1858 between the Russian Empire and the Qing Dynasty, Vladivostok was ceded to Russia. Even after World War II, the territory still remains in Russian hands. The Chinese name for Vladivostok is Haishenwai and is the capital of Primorsky Krai and is currently administered by Russia.

Of course, China is adamant that all territories taken in mid-nineteenth century should be returned to China. Former colonies of imperialists powers have to date return Macau and Hong Kong. China has made it clear that sooner or later Taiwan would also be reclaimed whether peacefully or even by force. Of late there are indications that China would also like the return of the Diaoyudao/Senkaku Islands. So far Japan does not appear willing to return the Senkaku Islands. There is no denying that the Diaoyudao/Senkaku Islands were once territories belonging to China. Further, Chinese animosities towards Japan is still an open sore. The atrocities and brutality it inflicted on the Chinese during the Sino-Japanese War from 1937 to 1945 is still fresh in the memories of those who survived the holocaust. The manner in which they raped, killed, and massacre the civilian population of Nanking ending in the tragic loss of 300,000 lives had been well documented. Those dark days of suffering and humiliations when the Japanese overrun the Chinese cities killing, raping, burning, sparing no civilian lives is still in the memories of those who survived the tragic invasion. And till this day, the Japanese have not shown remorse, nor admission of all the bloody deeds they did in the Second Sino-Japanese War from 1937 to 1945. And to add salt to the wound, Japan has not shown even the slightest compassion to return the Senkaku Islands they annexed from China in the course of their brutal invasion of China during the course of the Second Sino-Japanese War from 1937 to 1945.

Japan is wary of China's intention, fearing that one day China may resort to force to reclaim those islands. At the moment, the US has several military bases in Japan; and under security arrangements with the US, Japan feels secure of US protection. Even as recently, the US had assured Japan that ensuring their sovereignty over the Senkaku Islands was part of their security arrangements.

For their security and protection, Japan has joined the QUAD Alliance with India, Australia, and the US. This alliance has further angered China even more as the purpose was to contain and confront China rather than engage.

China has strengthened its naval power in the South China Seas and whether it will use diplomacy or force to reclaim those islands remain to be seen in the foreseeable future.

But Japan should not cling to those Senkaku Islands it had annexed during the Sino-Japanese War. Clinging to those annexed territories and hoping to have good relations with China is certainly incompatible. A solution to this contentious issue is for japan to return the Senkaku Islands it had annexed from China. As long as Japan refused to return those territories to China the underlying animosity will continue to fester.

Reference: More materials between China and Japan can be obtained below.

China Parts Ways with US, Japan Easy Money
While US Fed and BOJ pump trillions into markets the People's Bank of China is pursuing a more sensible monetary policy.
By William Pesek
December 11, 2020

Japan, Handed a 5G Lifeline by Trump's Crackdown on China's Huawei, Races to Catch Up

Japan lost its lead in consumer-facing handsets over the years and has fallen behind Nokia, Ericsson and Huawei in the buildout of 5G infrastructure

But with a US-led crackdown on China's Huawei, Japanese firms suddenly seem a lot more attractive to carriers around the world racing to upgrade their networks.

Bloomberg
Published: 10:12 a.m., December 11, 2020

Blunt Claim on Senkakus Overshadows Progress in China–Japan Meeting
By Satoshi Sugiyama
November 25, 2020

During an at times uneasy news conference in Tokyo, Beijing's foreign minister seemed determined to send a clear message over territorial disputes: China won't back down.

magazine with a *Diplomat All-Access* subscription.

CHINA AND INDONESIA

Despite frictions on unresolved conflicts in the South China Sea, China and Indonesia have seen growing cooperation on many fronts.

Despite the pandemic, Indonesia's coordinating minister for maritime affairs and investments, Luhut Binsar Pandjaitan, paid a visit to his Chinese counterpart, China's foreign affairs minister Wa Ying, to engage potential collaborations between the two countries.

One visible outcome of the meeting was to appoint Indonesia as the hub for distributing China's Covid-19 vaccines.

This arrangement ensured that China had a testing ground with Indonesia's population of 270 million and ensured China had access to the Southeast Asian market.

Such an arrangement would also ensure that Indonesia had priority to obtain the vaccine and any subsequent economic benefits.

China is currently Indonesia's second largest source of foreign direct investments (after Singapore) and its main trading partner. In 2019 China imported a value of US$25.8 billion which represents around 16.68% of Indonesia's total exports. For the same year, Indonesia imported from China worth US$44.5 billion which is almost a third of Indonesia's total imports. The bilateral trade signifies a growing close relationship between the two countries.

The two countries also agreed to use their respective currencies in their trade agreements thus abandoning the US dollar.

In addition, bilateral cultural exchanges, educational, and people-to-people exchanges were to be fostered.

The person most responsible for fostering good ties with Beijing is the former army general Luhut. He has visited Beijing several times and has been supportive of the Belt and Road Initiative.

He set up the Global Maritime Fulcrum Task Force and ensured the participation of various ministries and stakeholders to oversee the implementation of BRI projects in Indonesia.

The growing ties between the two countries will definitely benefit Indonesia in the coming decades. But this closeness with Beijing will damage its ties with the US. The recent request by US to allow its P-8 Poseidon maritime surveillance planes to land and refuel on Indonesian territory was flatly rejected. The P8 role was to monitor China's military activity in the South China Sea. Indonesia's reason for the rejection was that it wishes to remain neutral and does not wish to take sides in the geopolitical conflict between the two superpowers.

Indonesia did the right thing. The US and the Five Eyes nations do it all the time. They manufacture a crisis and demonize the country before giving an excuse to invade and punish them. They did it in Iraq; they did it in Vietnam, Afghanistan, Libya, and Syria. Then now they did it to Iran by assassinating their general Soleimani and recently also killing their prominent nuclear scientist, Mohsen Fakhrizadeh. All these provocations were to elicit a military response from Iran so that they will have an excuse to start a military conflict.

And with China they are doing precisely the same tactic. The US State Secretary goes round the world and tell everyone, China is a threat to democracy. They ply their warships and aircraft carriers sailing through the South China Sea under the guise of freedom of navigation. They fly their airplanes disguised as civilian planes to spy or eavesdrop on China. They do all these things and then say China is the aggressor.

But China should not allow their fishing vessels from trespassing in Indonesia's seas and Chinese coast guards should not encroach in Indonesia's territory. It is difficult to understand why China would allow such unnecessary skirmish to occur, causing needless tensions.

There is no territory dispute with Indonesia, and there is no reason why these clashes should occur with Indonesia.

China would only be driving all the Asean countries into US orbit and influence if China's action is regarded as a bully and an aggressor. As for now at least they have remained neutral, but for how long?

Reference: More reading articles can be obtained from the site below.

China–Indonesia Relations

Indonesian Special Envoy Visits China in Show of Cooperation
By Eleanor Albert
October 15, 2020

As Indonesia and China mark 70 years of relations, ties are marked by a tension between economic cooperation and ongoing maritime frictions.

The Internationalization of China's Currency in Indonesia
By Muhammad Zulfikar Rakhmat
July 31, 2020
The RMB is gradually making inroads in Indonesia.

The Complicated Politics of Chinese Workers in Indonesia
By Muhammad Zulfikar Rakhmat and Dikanaya Tarahita
June 26, 2020

The new wave of Chinese migrants has ignited criticism among many segments in Indonesian society—including Chinese Indonesians.

Why Isn't Indonesia Seeking China's Funding for Its New Capital?
By Muhammad Zulfikar Rakhmat and Dimas Permadi
April 03, 2020

Indonesia prefers to partner with other countries, not China, in building its new capital city. That's a wake-up call for Beijing.

Indonesia's Natuna Challenge
By Nabiha Shahab
March 13, 2020

Illegal fishing—including by Chinese vessels—continues to be a problem in the Natuna Sea.

Indonesia, China, and the Natuna Linchpin
By Evan A. Laksmana
March 01, 2020

Can Indonesia develop a strategy to confront China's long game in the Natunas and the South China Sea?

Coronavirus Takes Its Toll on China-Indonesia Relations
By Muhammad Zulfikar Rakhmat and Dikanaya Tarahita
February 15, 2020

Indonesia's travel ban could impact not only economic but political ties between the two countries.

Jokowi 2.0: Indonesia Amid US–China Competition
By Mercy A. Kuo
November 12, 2019

Insights from Bridget Welsh.

Understanding Indonesians' Souring Sentiment Toward China
By Dikanaya Tarahita and Muhammad Zulfikar Rakhmat
JUNE 6, 2019

Longstanding anti-Chinese prejudices, coupled with foreign policy fears, are bringing down China's image among Indonesians.

Chinese Culture Gradually Penetrates Indonesia
By Muhammad Zulfikar Rakhmat
April 18, 2019

Cultural activities are also a key part of the BRI, even though their influence remains limited so far.

The Belt and Road: The Good, the Bad, and the Mixed
By Angela Tritto and Alvin Camba
April 15, 2019

Demystifying China's Belt and Road Initiative through 3 case studies.

How Can Indonesia Take Advantage of the Belt and Road's Opportunities?
By Muhammad Zulfikar Rakhmat and Andry Satrio Nugroho
March 20, 2019

The BRI is a double-edged sword, how can Indonesia take advantage of the benefits and avoid the pitfalls?

CHINA VS. AUSTRALIA

In the 2007–2008 global financial crisis, Australia managed to escape unscathed when other economies were ravaged by the global financial crisis. Australia managed to ride out the storm because of its booming exports of iron ore and coal to China. And not long after that even surpassed Japan as the largest trading partner. And because of this, it was one of the few countries to avoid the economic downturn.

Fast-forward to May 2020, everything suddenly looked bleak. Trump was blaming China for the virus and even alleged that virus not only originated in China, but that it came from a bio lab that China had in Wuhan. Despite no evidence was produced and contrary to most scientists' opinion, Australia foolishly parroted Trump's narrative asking for the investigation into the origin of the virus in China. Little did the Australian PM recollect that early in February there was at least fifteen occasions that Trump was praising China's transparency and its ability to tackle the virus. However when events took a drastic turn and the virus death toll rose exponentially, Trump decided to play the blame game, and the Australian PM obediently followed Trump's narrative.

Unwittingly, he parroted Trump's call for an investigation of the origin of the virus in China. Naturally this infuriated the Chinese, and the ambassador came out with the statement that Chinese consumers could boycott Australian beef over Australia's persistent call for an international enquiry in the origin of the virus. The Chinese foreign ministry was of the view that it supported an inquiry at an appropriate time but would not let the issue to be politicized by US and some other countries based on the presumption of guilt.

Following the spat, the following Monday, Beijing informed the Australian government that they were suspending the imports of four Australian beef firms, and this was followed with the imposition of 80 percent tariffs on barley.

Coincidently, Australia's economy retreated into recession and consequently ended with two consecutive quarters of negative growth. The Australian GDP (gross domestic product) shrank 7 percent in the April to June quarter compared to the last three months. Treasurer Josh Frydenberg even told a press conference that the June quarter would see a staggering collapse of 20 percent.

Unlike the 2008 global financial crisis where Australia was the only major economy to avert a recession caused by the US subprime mortgage crisis. And the main reason for Australia's phenomenal economic growth was attributed solely to China's voracious appetite for its commodities such as coal, iron ore, and tourism which propelled Australia's incredible growth.

Such a glorious track record would have continued had not Scot Morrison, the PM of Australia, made the unthinkable mistake of picking a fight with Beijing, Australia's largest trading partners. Australia in April, relentlessly aided by US prodding, called for an international inquiry into the origins of the coronavirus. This angered the Chinese and accused Canberra for acting as the US "deputy sheriff" in the Asia Pacific region.

In May, China started to suspend imports from four major beef supplier for thirty days over alleged labelling issues. And this was followed by imposing an 80.5 percent of tariffs on all Australian barley grains. Later, trade tensions escalated to stringent customs inspection procedures on Australian iron ore imports.

Looking at the statistic, Australia's reliance on China's exports was mind boggling and not difficult to comprehend why China is its biggest trading partner. Australia's total export to China was A$135 billion annually providing a conduit for thousands of employment. Australian iron ore export to China in 2018–2019 was a record A$63 billion, added to natural gas of A$17 billion and A$14 billion of coal. In 2018–19 China imported over 2.5 million tons of Australian barley which constitute more than half of Australian barley exports. The imposition of 80.5 percent tariff on barley grain would cost the barley industry a loss of A$500 million per annum. In addition, Australia earned A$9.5 billion in beef export, non-beef meat (A$5.2 billion), wool (A$3.8 billion), and wheat (A$3.7 billion).

In June, China came out with a travel advisory for its country tourism and education sectors. They were advised to stay away from Australia because of racial incidents involving Asians residing in Australia. For the time being, the effect was minimal because the borders were still closed. However the education sector would see a loss of A$37.6 billion in education business. The travel advisory would cost tourism A$12 billion a year in revenue which translate to A$1 billion every month on its hotels, restaurants, tourism operator, and popular attractions.

In August, China initiated an "anti-dumping" investigation into imports of Australian wine. This resulted in anti-dumping tariffs of 202.70 percent which resulted in triple the price of Australian wine. The wine tariff was in retaliation for criticizing the new Hong Kong security law. The wine tariff would result in the loss of A$1.2 billion worth of wine a year.

Finally, on October 16, China gave instruction to its spinning mills to avoid buying Australian cotton. This could result in a loss of A$2.5 billion a year. This came one week after China's customs authorities told local steelmakers and power plants to stop importing Australian coal, resulting in a loss of A$14 billion to the industry.

China's engagement with Australia for their antagonistic attitude toward China is not only correct but a deserving response. Australia's PM Scott Morison's behavior is puzzling. On the one hand, he wants good trade relations with China, but on the hand, he wants to be US's pet poodle. Australia's strange demeanor toward China is nothing short of puzzlement. Thirty percent of its annual trade is with China, yet it has treated China with utter disdain. Instead of maintaining a cordial relationship, it has on several occasions deliberately by its action created unnecessary friction with its large beneficial trading partner.

Not only has it parroted US narrative that China's tech company Huawei was not safe and would not be safe security wise if they engage China to do their 5G network, following US directive, they disallowed China to be involved in the setting up of the 5G infrastructure and banned them from any installation of their network. This was despite the absence of any evidence that there was any backdoor in the Huawei's 5G network.

It then went further to pass an anti-foreign interference law and also expanded its powers to force the sale of foreign-owned businesses when it involves security issues.

Recently it even sent its warship to accompany US warships in the South China Seas ostensibly for the purpose of safeguarding freedom of navigation.

The last straw was when Australia joined the US in calling for an investigation of the origin of the virus in China.

One cannot understand how Australian foreign policies can be so servile to US interest though understandably they are united under the Five Eyes alliance. Is it not paramount that Australian foreign relations should foremost serve Australian interest rather than US interest?

Geographically, Australia is in Asia and not in the Gulf of Mexico, 6,000 miles away. Its vital interest is in Asia where it is located and not in the US sphere of influence. A question that should be in their minds is whether US can fill the $135 billion void that China trades with Australia. If not, then why is Australia treating China with such belligerence? Any student in foreign relations would conclude at the flaw manner in which Australia is handling their foreign relations with China. And really stupefying for Australia to express surprise and outrage for China applying sanctions on their beef and barley. How can they expect China to remain with elegant silence when there is no mutual respect from the Australian counterpart? China has every right to purchase their beef and barley from other sellers if Australian is behaving badly and treating with arrogance against China. Is this act by China any different from Trump's treatment of its trading partners with Mexico, Canada, France, and China? So why is Australia not critical of Trump's behavior? Australia's relations with China should from the outset be cordial and foster with mutual respect. Australia tend to forget that the buyer is always right. China does not have to buy Australia's goods. If Australia behaves badly, then China can take their business elsewhere, but can Australia fill the void that China leaves? If it can, well and good, but if it cannot, then it's time to eat humble pie and behave better with your prime customer and not be antagonistic. About time Australia take some basic lessons in foreign relations.

For clarity of the situation between Australia and China relations, I have included a few articles written by Australians critical of their government policies.

Two articles which best describe the current acrimonious spat was written by two writers and I prefer to append in toto their opinions.

The first article was written by David Scheer on May 22, 2020. The whole article is unedited and is well presented in its contents.

As China Diversifies Imports, Time Running Out for Australia
By Wang Bozun and Chu Daye
Source: *Global Times*
Published: June 22, 2020, 19:48:40

Time Running Out for Canberra to Fix Ties with Beijing: Analysts

---

Diplomacy
China–Australia Relations: Could New Zealand Show the Way to Better Ties?

- Chinese foreign minister calls for signing of upgrade to free-trade agreement in call with New Zealand counterpart
- The two countries are an example for others to follow, he says

China Economy
China–Australia Relations: Could Wool, Honey, Fruit, Dairy or Pharmaceutical Products Be Next in the Crosshairs?

- Australian wool exporters have limited alternative markets, and 'a substantive barrier would cripple the Australian industry'
- A new analysis by research house IBISWorld also shows that a raft of products could be targeted by Beijing due to their reliance on the Chinese market for export sales

Diplomacy
China–Australia Relations: Global Times Accused of 'Inflammatory' Coverage

- Tabloid boss Hu Xijin reports Australian ambassador told him his country does not follow the US on all China-related issues
- Department of Foreign Affairs and Trade says newspaper's account is inaccurate

TOP PICKS
Top Canadian Border Officer Denies Destroying Meng Wanzhou Documents
December 12, 2020

China, Australia and the Big Questions Over a Papua New Guinea Fishing Hub
By Australian ABC radio host

OPINION
Peter Goers: With China, many Aussies are absolute hypocrites.

"Revolution is just a T-shirt away," sings Billy Bragg. The T-shirts are made in China like everything else. We wear and consume the proof of the success of the Chinese Revolution and they drink our wine, use our iron ore, eat our tucker and enrich our entire tourism and education sectors.

Carr, who served under Abbott's rival and predecessor Kevin Rudd as a member of the center-left Labor Party, said Canberra was correct to pursue "a pragmatic, national-interest based policy on China."

"We take that alliance very seriously, it's one of the three foundations of Australian foreign policy," he said. "We are still capable of difference with the Americans when we assert an Australian national interest."

Carr said he did not disagree with Canberra's stance on points of contention with Beijing such as Huawei and the need for an international inquiry into the coronavirus pandemic, but the current government had been ham-fisted in its approach to diplomacy.

Loss of Chinese Buyers: Final Straw for Australia's Property Market?
July 20, 2020

Australian exports to China hit a record A$14.6 billion (US$10.4 billion) in June, fueled by imports of iron ore and coal as Beijing sought to kick-start economic growth following the lifting of coronavirus lockdowns across the country. The share of exports to China reached an all-time of 48.8 per cent, despite Beijing this year slapping restrictions on Australian beef and barley. The trade measures were widely seen in Australia as retaliation for Canberra's push for an independent international inquiry into the origins of the pandemic.

07:34
Australia And China Cooperation Too Valuable for 'Nonsensical' Decoupling

'EPICENTRE OF STRATEGIC COMPETITION'

On Tuesday, Australian Prime Minister Scott Morrison told the Aspen Security Forum in Colorado that the region was an "epicenter of strategic competition," and building an alliance of like-minded countries would be a "critical priority."

Both Abbott and Carr warned of the increasing risk of military conflict between Washington and Beijing in the South China Sea or the Taiwan Strait.

Australian Prime Minister Scott Morrison. Photo: EPA

"There's an immediate task on Australia and other nations and that is to exercise what influence we can with both sides about bringing them back from the brink," said Carr, saying the Bornean state will "always be part of Malaysia."

Bhavan Jaipragas
Published: 10:45 p.m., August 5, 2020

Why you can trust SCMP
1.5k

Image: Shutterstock

Malaysia on Wednesday warned that the South China Sea dispute that has emerged as a key proxy battle between the US and China could split the Asean bloc if countries gave in to the superpowers' "narratives and pressure" over the row.

John Power
Published: 9:30 p.m., August 5, 2020

China suspends Hong Kong extradition treaties with Canada, Australia, UK
Sea claims

Why Australia Is Spending Big on Weapons Against a 'Rising China'

The paper claims Australia is "not as tactful" as its Five Eyes alliance partners the United Kingdom and Canada, accusing the Morrison Government of aggressively following Washington's lead against China.

Must Australia choose between trade with China and siding with US on Hong Kong, South China Sea?

Canberra has signaled it will not join Washington in a new cold war with Beijing—sceptics wonder if it has any alternative Australia is one of America's staunchest security allies, but alienating its largest trade partner would cost it dear.

Zhou Xin

China's Handling of Australia Row Highlights What May Be an Increasingly Hard Line in Diplomatic Affairs

- Speech by vice-minister of foreign affairs offers a hint at the future of Chinese diplomacy
- Through Australia, China is setting the record straight—there will be consequences for offending Beijing

CHINA AND UNITED KINGDOM

Britain should look closely at its past before passing judgements on countries like China. Britain has left behind a legacy of atrocities in practically every continent it colonized. The present generation of British citizens should be aware of its past history so that they should acknowledge the litany of atrocities they committed in all the countries they colonized in the early eighteenth, nineteenth, and twentieth centuries. No wonder they were called the "Evilest Empire."

During the prevalent slavery period, Britain was the most aggressive and vicious trader of African American slaves. American Natives were butchered poisoned, and the British colonizer perpetuated a policy of exterminating the natives so that they could steal their land. The cruelty to the Native/Aboriginal Americans extended to the use of germ warfare by "gifting" pox-infected blankets. The British even "scalped heads" and paid rewards and bounties for Indian scalps in order to wipe them out.

In 1788 the British invaded and colonized Australia and for the next two hundred years began a period of aboriginal genocide. As a jovial pastime, they would decapitate aboriginal babies by kicking their heads. In the name of science, Britain decapitated aborigines and Maoris' heads and shipped them back to British museums.

From 1900 to 1970s, white Australia kidnapped thousands of aboriginal children and gave to white families for adoptions—they were called the stolen generations.

Under UN definition, such forced adoption constitutes genocide, but till today no white British or Australian has been prosecuted for genocidal crimes.

In the twentieth century Britain caused the starvation of over 5 million Bengalese. And in Africa, British plundered and raped the country for five hundred years. Its resources were plundered, stripped, and shipped to Britain. And today, British legacy is self-evident as the country lays in ruins and devastation, ravaged by famines and conflicts—a gruesome legacy of British imperialism.

In the nineteenth century, Britain forced China under the Treaty of Nanking to allow them to sell opium to the Chinese people. The British Empire was the biggest drug pusher of that era, and as a result, Hong Kong was ceded to the British for 150 years. The irony of it all was that when it was returned to China in 1997, they had the gall to stipulate the conditions that China had to adhere as a precondition for the return. Hong Kong should have long ago returned to China and not for the duration of 150 years. The Treaty of Nanking which resulted from the opium war was legally and morally wrong and its ensuing treaty should have been declared void. For Britain to criticize China's lack of freedom and human rights violation when for its entire period of British rule no universal suffrage was granted to the Hongkongers.

In view of all the above past atrocities committed by the British imperialist, what right does it has to point its bloodstained fingers at China or other countries for human right violations? For a long time, the British has been able to conceal their massive criminality against humanity and perhaps it's time the world should now know the past atrocities committed by Imperial Britain in all its gory and infamy.

British hypocrisy is so obvious when it criticized China for legislating the security law for Hong Kong. Can the UK government deny that they do not have a security law that forbids treason, terrorism, and consorting with foreign powers to the detriment of its national interest?

The British government is practicing double standard. For over 150 years of their rule in Hong Kong, they did not grant universal suffrage and all important posts were not even elected. They were appointed from London. If they had not given Hong Kong during that period of their rule, why are they now demanding such freedom for Hong Kong? In fact under the present "one country, two system"' policy, Hong Kong was given more freedom than ever been given under British rule.

British Foreign Secretary Dominic Raab's assertion that the solution to the city's unrest and disturbances should come from the Hong Kong legislature and not from Beijing. But this is a moot point since 2003, the Hong Kong legislature had not been able to pass any such security laws because of street protests and strong opposition from certain sections of the lawmakers. Raab further threatened that the British government would put in place and allow certain British National (oversea status) to work and study over an extended one-year period. The solution for China is simple. Since the British government is so concerned for the lack of freedoms and values in Hong Kong for its citizens, then let the British government take all those Hong Kong British Nationals to their country. China should be happy to unload these rebellious citizens who have been causing the violence and disturbance in the Chinese enclave. If they can be disloyal to their own mother country, let us see how loyal and patriotic they can be to their adopted British masters.

The British government has failed to grasp the historical nature of how Hong Kong was ceded to the British under the unequal treaties signed in 1842. The humiliation, subjugation, and oppression the Chinese endured are still fresh in their memories. By handing over and signing the joint Declarations Agreement in 1993 does not bestow them any legal right to dictate to China how they should govern their own territory. Any attempt to criticize or persuade China how it should formulate its policy with regards to security, terrorism, and consorting with foreign powers to subvert Hong Kong are viewed as interference of China's internal affairs. Foreign Secretary Dominic Raab would do well to position itself in the same position if China were to intervene in the British government internal or domestic affairs. It is totally against international norms for any country to interfere in the internal affairs of another country.

The British government should not be constantly acting and parroting what US does or what it wants the British government to do. It should be able to independently assess the situation in Hong Kong and make its own judgement devoid of any instigation from their Five Eyes allies. The violence perpetuated by the protestors in Hong Kong are no longer peaceful. They have resorted to arbitrary destruction of public and private properties, committing arson, assaulting civilians who did not agree with their views and consorting with foreign powers to destabilize Hong Kong. All these acts no western countries would neither condone nor allow. Further, all these countries have similar security laws to protect the security and sovereignty of their own countries, yet through sheer hypocrisy, they can oppose China from legislating such laws.

The UK PM Boris Johnson resorted to withdrawing the extradition treaty with Hong Kong and vowed to amend the country's immigration law to enable millions of Hongkongers a path to British citizenship if China persisted with the controversial security law for the city.

Naturally, China reacted angrily and issued the statement through their Foreign Minister, Wang Yi, that "the Hong Kong

Matters are purely China's internal affairs and we do not allow external interference. Safeguarding national security in Hong Kong is China's core interest and an important principle we must adhere to."

Frankly, why should China worry if UK is prepared to take in those rebellious, violent Hongkongers who wished to immigrate to UK? China should be happy if UK is prepared to give sanctuary to these violent activists who were prepared to betray their own motherland. Imagine if these people can betray their own country then perhaps one day they could also betray their adopted country. So for those Hongkongers who wish to immigrate, Beijing should just offload them. Obviously, UK, under pressure from US, was merely parroting their support under the Five Eyes alliance which included, Canada, Australia, and New Zealand. Their opposition to the Hong Kong Security Law was sheer hypocrisy. For almost one year, violent demonstrations in the city state had brought the former colony to a grinding halt and its economy was badly affected by the frequent violent demonstrations. The security law was to address subversion, secession, collusion with foreign forces, and such laws were similar to the laws that all the Five Eyes countries had. It was clearly double standard practiced by the Five Eyes countries. Further, Hong Kong was without question a territory of China, and they had every right to enact what law they deemed necessary to bring law and order to the city state. What right had other countries poking their nose in the internal affairs of China? In fact, the onus of implementing Article 23 was entrusted to the Hong Kong government, but their failure to fulfil their obligations led to the central government to implement Article 23 via the security law.

In one stroke, UK exited from the European Union consisting of twenty-seven countries, had a woeful relation with Russia, and took to breaking relations with China by banning them from doing infrastructure 5G networks under the pretext of security concerns. But for the most part of their 3G and 4G networks, China was fully involved with their installations. So why the sudden security concerns which was not there before? Quite obviously under pressure from the US, Boris finally acquiesced to ban Huawei from being involved with the 5G infrastructure works.

One would have thought that after exiting from Brexit, UK would be looking to have better relations with China, the second largest economy. But alas, UK was going in the opposite direction as far as their relations with China was concerned.

THE DIPLOMAT

DIPLOMACY
UK–China Relations: From Gold to Dust

The rapid recent souring of British perceptions of China has as much to do with domestic factors as American pressure.

By Thomas des Garets Geddes
October 2, 2020

Why Are UK and China Relations Getting Worse?
By Christopher Giles
BBC News
Published: July 20, 2020

China–U.K. Relations Grow More Strained Over Huawei and Hong Kong
Publication: *China Brief*, volume 20, issue 15
By Taylor Butch
Published: August 31, 2020, 04:08 p.m.
Age: 3 months

THE FINANCIAL TIMES

UK–China Relations: From 'Golden Era' to the Deep Freeze

Bilateral ties have been deteriorating, but a rejection of Huawei by Britain would mark a new low.

UK Plans Cut in Huawei's 5G Network Involvement: Report

The development would mark a change of direction for Britain, which had earlier decided to allow Huawei in the non-sensitive parts of the country's 5G mobile network.

Prime Minister Boris Johnson plans to reduce China's involvement in British infrastructure to zero by 2023, the report said.

CHINA AND TAIWAN

To understand Taiwan's position in the present world, one must understand its historical context. Taiwan will not and never will be an independent country. Historically and geographically it is part of China. And no intelligent person would argue otherwise. It would be plain foolish for any leader to consider Taiwan as an independent state. To even declare independence by Taiwan would be suicidal.

The present Taiwan government is under the illusion that someday with US backing it will be able to gain independence and be a separate sovereign country. Realistically that cannot happen, and the sooner the leaders and its people accept this reality, the better and safer for its future prosperity.

China from the very beginning has already made it clear that Taiwan is an unalienable part of China and one day either through peaceful means or force it is inevitable that there will be a reunification of the two states. This is a core issue that China will not compromise, and the sooner the US and the West realize this reality, the better it will be for world peace. By encouraging Taiwan to rebel and seek independence is looking for a military conflict against China. It is certainly incomprehensible why US should want Taiwan to break away and be an independent country. The only possible reason is to destabilize China and to hopefully establish a military base on the front of China's territory. Would China allow this? Yes if US would also allow China to establish a military base in Cuba with missiles aiming at the US.

For the sake of world peace, US should in fact support the peaceful unification of Taiwan and China rather than encouraging Taiwan to be a breakaway province. Selling arms and initiating bilateral relations with Taiwan is certainly a hostile behavior that may only result in a military conflict between the two superpowers. Instead US should hold to the agreement of a One China policy which has been the bedrock of understanding since Nixon started relations with China in 1978.

The Taiwanese government is so foolish to spend billions on buying obsolete arms from the US thinking it would be able to protect itself against China. And Taiwan is under false illusion that its defense treaty with America would be adequate protection for them. One thing Taiwan and Asian countries have to realize is that America will not and cannot go to war with China in order to protect them. They abandoned the Vietnamese in Saigon and South Vietnam was handed over to Ho Chi Minh. In Syria they abandoned the Kurds when they exited from Syria. When asked by reporters, Trump replied that they did not help the Allied forces fight in Normandy, so why should I help them.? These words should ring fear in South Korea and Japan if they had not still realized the implications. Korea and Japan did not help the Allied forces in Normandy. So would American soldiers fight and die to defend Korea or Japan? Obviously no. Japan and Korea would be wiser if they maintain and build good relations with neighboring countries especially China rather than depending on American help in times of crisis.

Taiwan is merely living on borrowed time. Only matter of time when it will return to China's fold. It would be wiser if Taiwan leaders realize this reality. There is no way even with

America's support that Taiwan can gain independence and be an independent state. Further, the long-term prosperity of Taiwan would require considerable amount of support and goodwill from China. And it would be plain foolish for Taiwanese leaders to even think they could exist without China's support. Proximity and geographically speaking Taiwan should realize that their future and well-being is with China and not with America which is 6,000 miles away in the Gulf of Mexico. For its long-term prosperity and stability, it would be in their interest to remain align to China then be in constant conflict.

In fact the propose one country, two systems principle would be an attractive proposition for Taiwan. Taiwan leaders should wisely adopt this system and be part of China. Realistically, Taiwan is in Asia and not in the Gulf of Mexico. Taiwan should realize that its future is brighter if they return and be part of China rather being antagonistic toward China.

Reference: More materials can be obtained from the site below.

US Plans to Sell More Drones, Missiles to Taiwan: Report

Administration proposes sale of more sophisticated weaponry to the self-ruled island as China ratchets up pressure.

China Launches 'Grey-Zone' Warfare to Subdue Taiwan

South China Sea: Beijing Doubles Down After US Sails Through Waters

Trouble is reaching fever pitch in the South China Sea as Beijing doubles down on what they've called "provocative actions" by the US.

October 14, 2020, 8:39 a.m.

Attack on Taiwan an Option to Stop Independence, Top China General Says
By Yew Lun Tian

China/Diplomacy
Explainer: US-China-Taiwan: How Will Joe Biden Change the Balance?

- Taiwanese President Tsai Ing-wen was among the first to tweet her congratulations to Joe Biden and Kamala Harris
- The US president-elect is expected to walk a fine line that offers support to Taipei but does not antagonize Beijing

THE DEATH OF US RESERVE CURRENCY

When Nixon made the deal with Saudi Arabia for all oil purchase to be transacted in US dollar, the general consensus was its function was to serve as a reserve currency and not as a weapon to punish countries that did not agree with the US. However, of late, the US has been using the reserve currency as a weapon to punish countries that did not behave to US liking. Thus we see Iran, Russia, and Venezuela were all applied sanction by the American financial system. Lately, because of Hong Kong's security law, some of its leaders were also sanctioned in terms of dealing with banks.

Needless to say, this has caused a lot of fear and anger by the US action of using the reserve currency as a weapon.

However, with the recent withdrawal from international obligations and the substantial weakening of its domestic economy, there is a realistic expectation that the dollar could erode gradually. The pandemic has pushed the Central Bank to finance fiscal stimulus to the tune of US$ 11 trillion, thus ballooning government debt to a mind-boggling US$70 trillion (according to Institute of International Finance).

With the gradual decline in the value of the dollar, markets will see a shift to buying precious metals and non-dollar currencies. In tandem with the fall of the dollar global reserves, trade, banking, financial transactions and commodities could also simultaneously decline.

Two important factors could also contribute to the demise of the US dollar. One is the introduction of the digital currency by China. The digital currency is currently under trial in four cities: the Xiongan New Area in north China's Hebei Province, Shenzhen in south China's Guangdong Province, SuZhou in east China's Jiangsu Province, and Chengdu in southwest China's Sichuan Province. In addition, it will also be tested during the 2022 Winter Olympics Games in Beijing.

The next factor could be caused by the introduction of electric cars which will soon replace cars using fossil oil. With the advent of electric cars, the need to purchase oil no longer exist, and with this, the need to use dollar for oil will cease to exist. Thus countries no longer need to have dollars for the purchase of oil and hence the demand for dollar will diminish.

In August 1971, Nixon closed the gold window and virtually destroyed the currency system. In the same year, China predicted the US economic crisis and the collapse of the capitalist monetary system. In monetary terms, the dollar has declined 98 percent against gold and 78 percent against the Swiss Franc. With the collapse of the American dollar and its economy, a new superpower, China, will emerge.

THE FALL OF THE US EMPIRE			
	1969	2020	CHANGE
US Federal debt	$360 billion	$27 trillion	Up 75x
US total debt	$1.5 trillion	$81 trillion	Up 53x
US GDP	$1 trillion	$20 trillion	Up 20x
US debt to GDP	35%	135%	Up 4x
CHINA GDP	$80 billion	$14 trillion	Up 175x
Dow Jones	800	27,170	Up 34x
Gold	$35	$1,860	Up 53x
US$ vs Gold	$35	$1,860	Down 98%
US$ vs Swiss Franc	4.30	0.927	Down 79%

Table and figures taken from an extract of Egon Von Greyerz's article "King of World News."

From the above table, you will notice that US GDP had shot up from 35% in 1969 to 135% in 2020, which is up four times. Whereas China had gone up from $80 billion up to $14 trillion, which is up 175 times. With such a high level of debt, future growth is difficult. With the decline in tax revenue and an increase in expenditure, it will be difficult to introduce monetary policy that will reduce its debts. In the event of interest rates going up, the government will have difficulty in servicing its debts let alone settling its principals. This will result in a debt default and the collapse of the US economy.

With the current pandemic which necessitate the introduction of monetary stimulus, the US debt will increase by a few trillions. And with Trump's policy of reducing corporation tax thus reducing tax revenue and increasing expenditure, the US GDP will balloon to almost $80 trillion. Based on these figures, it is very likely a debt default is looming for the US economy and most likely will be in the coming years.

Commentary: America's Mountain of Debt Is a Ticking Time Bomb https://newswav.com/A2008_fEQTTK?s=A_ Scba2bz

How at Risk Is the USD of Losing Its Status as Global Reserve Currency?

For nearly a century, the USD has held its position as the world's trusted reserve currency, replacing the role previously held by the GBP. The future of the dollar as the most popular reserve currency has become increasingly uncertain in recent months.

Investors seek to hold a basket of investments rather than a single stock, central banks are also keen to do so when it comes to managing their reserves.

Stephen Roach

Why the US Dollar Is Only Going to Fall Faster and Harder

Given the unprecedented erosion of domestic savings, an explosive current account deficit, and the Fed determined to keep rates flat, expect the dollar to plunge by as much as 35 percent next year.

This will trigger a collapse in the US current-account deficit. Lacking savings and wanting to invest and grow, the US must import surplus savings and run massive external deficits to attract foreign capital.

This was confirmed by recently released second-quarter international transactions statistics. Reflecting the savings plunge, the US current-account deficit widened to 3.5 percent of GDP—the worst since the 4.3 percent deficit in the fourth quarter of 2008.

This widening of the deficit by 1.4 percentage points from the previous quarter is the largest deterioration since records started in 1960. Like the savings collapse, the current-account dynamic is unfolding in ferocious fashion.

America is facing an unprecedented wave of bankruptcies. It must act now

Project Syndicate
From our archive

This article appeared in the *South China Morning Post* print edition as "No End in Sight to the Decline in Dollar."

Stephen S. Roach, a faculty member at Yale University and former chairman of Morgan Stanley Asia, is the author of *Unbalanced: The Codependency of America and China.*

Opinion
Macroscope by David Brown

Why US Dollar Bears Should Watch Out for November's Presidential Election

The dollar is being undermined by loose US monetary policy and uncertainty surrounding the outcome of the poll. The latter could mark a turning point for the currency

While Trump should manage the dollar in a globally responsible manner, Beijing has plenty of scope to target a weaker renminbi while inflation risks remain low.

MF Admits China Has Overtaken the US as the World's Largest Economy; But Why Is the Media Silent?

Published: October 18, 2020
By EurAsian Times Desk

The world is waking up to a new reality post the devastating pandemic that brought everything to a grinding halt. One of them is the rise of China as the undisputed new economic superpower.

COVID-19, Political Fights Raise the Question: Could the Dollar Lose Its Global Status?
Paul Davidson

USA TODAY

In the most uncertain era of our lives, there are still a few sure things: Death. Taxes. And the dollar's status as the world's reserve currency.

On second thought, you might want to strike that last one.

Low interest rates
The prospect of higher inflation
Ballooning US debt
Fed money-printing

The Fed is expected to buy nearly $3 trillion in treasuries and mortgage-backed securities this year to ensure those markets function smoothly and to hold down long-term interest rates. But to make those purchases, which keep borrowing costs low for the federal government, the Fed effectively prints money. That substantially increases the supply of dollars and lowers their value.

Widening trade deficit

The US already had a big trade deficit, especially with China. During the crisis, exports have fallen more sharply than imports, in part because the US reopened its economy earlier than other countries, leading to a bigger rebound in US purchases of foreign goods. When imports exceed exports, more dollars leave the country and are converted into other currencies.

CHINA'S STRATEGY TO DEFLECT WESTERN HOSTILITY

US and its Western allies especially the Five Eyes will not allow China to expand economically and militarily to become a global power. Their strategy is plain and consistent. They will never praise China for whatever China does even though it is right and beneficial. To do so would be an admission of superiority of China's ideological system. That itself would tantamount to say China's system was far superior to the Western model which incorporates a liberal democracy.

Under the Trump administration, US Secretary of State Mike Pompeo's frequently rant that China is a threat to global peace and that they harbor a desire to dominate the world. This unfortunately is a false narrative. The truth is China's pattern of behavior and priorities since 1978 has been consistent. With its economic growth, admittedly, China became more assertive internationally. But the country that defied international norms and trampled on the rules of the global order was the US.

US is not satisfied with China's expansion in the American diaspora. Under the guise of security issue, it banned China's Huawei from building their 5G infrastructure network. Not satisfied with banning the Chinese tech China from operating in the US, it went further to persuade its Five Eyes allies to also ban China from the respective allied countries.

With such hostile reactions from these Western countries, China should now change its strategy. China should stop selling its advance 5G technology to all these Western countries. China has the most advanced 5G technology. Its nearest competitor is two years behind in terms of developing a 5G system which costs more than what China can offer. It does not have to persuade countries to install this latest 5G equipment. It should just concentrate on installing and developing 5G base stations in the whole of rural and urban China, thus providing state-of-the-art 5G technology for the whole country. The West can only look with envy when China has a vast network of 5G state-of-the-art internet system. After having seen what China has done, these countries will come running to China begging for it to be installed in their country. When you have a product that is advanced and economical, you don't have to worry about buyers. Marketing principles dictate they will come knocking at your door.

There is a current consensus among Western nations that China's wolf warriors in trade sanctions especially against Australia has backfired. The trade sanctions by China will not work. To show solidarity for Australian wines that was virtually banned by China because of high tariffs, these countries banded and bought wines from the Australian winery. The sheer evidence of hypocrisy is seen here. Why did this nation not show the same level of support for China when US, UK, and Australia banned the 5G network of Huawei which was banned by these countries? Why did they not respond and give Huawei the same support they gave to Australia, a Western Caucasian country? Or are they implying that it's all right to ban an Asian product but it's not all right for an Asian country to ban a Western product?

China's action of trade reprisal against countries acting against its interest is correct. Why should China support by buying from countries who constantly act against its interest like Australia? Surely China has the prerogative to select trading with friendly countries as against countries that are hostile toward its interest.

China's Leading Spot in the Race for Technological Innovation
By Matteo Giovannini

Editor's note: Matteo Giovannini is a finance professional at the Industrial and Commercial Bank of China in Beijing and a member of the China Task Force at the Italian Ministry of Economic Development. The article reflects the author's opinions and not necessarily the views of CGTN.

Why China Is Taking Over the 'American Century'

Instead of recouping its former technological prowess, the US relies on China-bashing and tech bans.

By Dilip Hiro
Published: August 19, 2020

The founder of Alibaba, Jack Ma, was at the forefront of China's rise on the technological stage. Photo: AFP / Minasse Wondimu Hailu / Anadolu Agency

For the Trump administration's senior officials, it has been open season on bashing China. If you need an example, think of the president's blame game about "the invisible Chinese virus" as it spreads wildly across the US.

WILL US AND CHINA GO TO WAR?

Ever since 2018, the US under Trump has been blaming China for their trade deficit. After some lengthy acrimonious negotiation between the two parties, a final trade settlement was drafted and agreed by both parties. That was only the beginning of tensions which was slowly brewing between the two superpowers. In early 2019, the Canadian government under directions from US detained the financial executive of the tech giant Huawei for breach of sanctions against Iran and banking fraud. This was followed with the banning of Huawei from being involved in the infrastructure development of 5G in the US, ostensibly for security reasons.

In mid June of 2020, Trump ordered the closure of the Houston Embassy, giving three days' notice. And the Chinese retaliated by closing the American Embassy in Chengdu. This was followed by the nonrenewal of Chinese journalists' visa to work in the US for reason that they were security risks. In August, Trump went further by signing an executive order to ban a social media tech giant called TikTok and WeChat. In order to avoid a ban, the tech giant had to sell the TikTok app to a US company named Microsoft. The executive order for the sale by Trump was subsequently complicated by the Chinese government to disallow the sale of Chinese tech unless permission was obtained for export sale of any Chinese tech company.

The continuous onslaught of Chinese tech companies and the frequent racists calling for the Wuhan and Chinese virus by Trump deliberately demonize China in every way possible. Perhaps it was his strategy to use China as his bogeyman to help him divert his failure in controlling the pandemic. In August, US Secretary of Health paid a visit to Taiwan ostensibly to study their capability in overcoming the virus. All these actions by the US was deliberate provocations by the US to ignite a military conflict. Perhaps it was the realization that America's global hegemony was threatened by China who would topple them in due course. At the moment, in Washington, there is a bipartisan consensus that China poses an existential threat to world peace and a threat to America's hegemony.

Things came to a head in August when the Chinese NPC (National People's Congress) passed a security law for Hong Kong which would outlaw subversion, call for independence, and collusion with foreign governments as offences under the proposed act. This quickly earned the wrath of US and his Five Eyes Allies which immediately cancelled their respective extradition treaty with Hong Kong. The anger elicited by the US government was obvious. For the past year, Hong Kong was enveloped in violent street demonstrations initially caused by a proposed extradition treaty to bring a murderer from Taiwan. However, because of strong public protest, the extradition treaty did not see the light of day. Despite the shelving of the proposed extradition treaty, the violent street demonstrations continued. It became quite obvious to Hong Kong and Beijing leaders that foreign elements were supporting the demonstrations. CIA operatives using the NED (National Endowment for Democracy) was financing the violent street demonstrations, some calling for independence and some activists were travelling to the US calling for the sanctions of Hong Kong leaders. This was clearly Hong Kong citizens colluding with foreign powers to impose sanctions on the Hong Kong government.

As a result of the Hong Kong Security Law passed by the NPC, the US withdrew the extradition treaty and also cancelled the special trade status of Hong Kong. In addition, Trump also imposed sanctions on officials from Xinjiang for human rights violation.

On a more enlightening note, one should note the sheer hypocrisy of the US and Five Eyes allies. They were against China for passing a security law for Hong Kong despite the necessity for such a law. The violent demonstrators were committing arson on public property. They were publicly advocating for independence and flying the stars and stripes and the Union Jack. They were publicly colluding with foreign powers to punish Hong Kong. This was clearly treason, and no Western government would tolerate such behaviors of their own citizens, yet they can shamefully object to China passing such a security law.

Then on human rights violations, the US and UK government should firstly be aware of their own failure to observe human rights. They should own and accept their human rights violations in all the countries they colonized. How shameful of them to preach to others about Uyghur human rights violations when their own history is replete with abundant atrocities committed by their own imperialist governments. They should be aware of their own vile and evil human rights violations which were far more cruel and inhuman than what China is putting the Uyghurs in camps to train them in professional jobs.

US Secretary of State said they would impose visa restrictions on Chinese firms like Huawei that he accused of facilitating human rights violations. That is akin to any country saying that Amazon, an American company, should be punished for doing business because US has killed millions of civilians in Afghanistan, Iraq, Libya, Syria, and Vietnam. Is that not US warmongering history? And what about millions of homeless people wandering in American streets, say, in San Francisco? The US should be the last country to preach about human rights when their own history is littered with many human rights violations.

Further its common knowledge that China does not allow Facebook and Twitter to operate in China but instead have their own social media like Weibo, Youku, Douyin and WeChat. But do you see the Chinese government officials go round the world to bully and tell the world to ban and not use Facebook or Twitter? No, the Chinese government didn't do that. US behavior is typical of its imperial legacy.

The irony of the situation is that the US Secretary of State Mike Pompeo has been telling the world that China was a threat to the world. He ranted that Beijing's governance, economic system, espionage activities, and handling of the pandemic were the source of threat to the world. But who is really the threat? US or China? Since the beginning of mid July of 2018, the US had been imposing tariffs which were against WTO rules. And from then onward, the US had been endlessly finding fault with China on various issues starting with the pandemic when the Covid-19 virus in Wuhan was detected. Initially, Trump heaped praise in January on the Chinese transparency and ability to overcome the virus. But gradually when Trump failed to control and suppress the spread of the virus, he started to direct the blame on the Chinese government under Xi Jing Peng.

To those who are familiar with US warmongering behavior, it was quite obvious the aggressor was not China but the US. How could China be a threat to global peace when it has not gone to war in forty years (except with Vietnam in 1979), whereas US has been the warmongering nation? They were sending warships, destroyers, aircraft carriers to the South China Sea causing tensions to the area. Why should the US act as if they were the appointed policeman of the world? Their country is in the Gulf of Mexico which is 6,000 miles away. Why should they send their armada of ships to the South China Sea in a threatening manner? And this act of aggression certainly would provoke China to respond by also sending their warships to ensure their territory was safe from any foreign intrusion. And what if the situation was reversed and China was to send its warship to the Gulf of Mexico? Would the US accept it as threatening their country, or would they treat it as normal? Further, the US has been building bases in the South China Seas with fortified military missiles aimed at China. This itself was an aggressive move which can be construed as an attempt to intimidate China. Would the US allow such aggression on its doorstep? Of course not, and they are precisely doing it and then labelling China as the aggressor. From the manner in which the US foreign policy is being conducted, the one obvious strategy of the US is to first demonize China in every way possible. This was similar to the strategy adopted before the invasion of Iraq. The US told the world that Iraq was building weapon of mass destruction and the country was a threat to world peace. The same strategy and narrative is now being paraded to demonize China and then later perhaps to create a plot to ignite a military conflict.

So far, Australia has been vocal in support of US accusation of an assertive and aggressive China. And in retaliation, China has imposed a high tariffs on its barley and a total ban on beef and wine imports from Australia. The South China Sea nations who have allowed US to build military bases in their territory should heed the warning that there is a price to pay for their support of US militarism. Allowing US to build military bases is akin to complicit in the plot to attack China in the event of a military conflict. And it pays to realize that should any conflict arise, these military bases are first targets to be destroyed even at the cost of civilian lives. China will certainly not allow these military bases to be the launching pads of missile strikes on Chinese territories. As much as these bases have missile aimed at China, you can be rest assured that there are also missiles from China aimed strategically at the South China bases hosting American military complex. On hindsight, of course it pays to be neutral like the following countries that do not host any US military base: Singapore, Malaysia, Thailand, and Indonesia. Countries like Japan, Korea, Philippines unfortunately will be first target to be stricken in the event of a US–China military conflict.

There is no doubt that US is looking for a war with China. Its warships and aircraft carriers having been sailing the South China Sea under the guise of freedom of navigation. China has never blocked or prevented navigation along the South China Seas. So why is US parading its warships in the South China Sea? Freedom of navigation is for commercial vessels and certainly not warships, destroyers, and aircraft carriers. Would US feel threatened if China was to send its warships and carriers to the Gulf of Mexico to also ensure freedom of navigation?

To increase further enmity between the two countries, US sends over their health minister to Taiwan under the pretext of studying how Taiwan dealt successfully with the pandemic. And of late, the US State Department has declared they will be selling missiles and other arms to Taiwan. All these acts are deliberate provocations with intent for China perhaps to start some military response.

US should stop interfering in China's territorial dispute with Taiwan. Taiwan historically is part of China. Instead of encouraging Taiwan for a peaceful reunification with China, it is trying to drive a wedge between China and Taiwan. Selling arms to Taiwan was only encouraging a military conflict between a territory deemed a part of China.

The sad part is that Western countries like the Five Eyes alliance with US have never spoken out against US's deliberate act of provocations. Instead, countries like UK, Canada, and Australia have been acting in concert to demonize China as the aggressor and that US was merely acting a world policeman.

It is reassuring to know that China has declared it will not fire the first bullet to start a war. But with US blatant provocations, any small spark could ensue a military conflict which may not have been intended. Any major conflict between the two superpowers would be catastrophic to the world, and unless the other Five Eyes countries stop supporting US's deliberate provocations, there is no guarantee a military conflict between the two superpowers can be averted.

China's strategy of containment of any US provocations and aggression should be pragmatic and simple. China does not seek any military confrontation with the US knowing fully well that they cannot match US in a head on military conflict. All China has to do is to bid its time. US is seriously mired in 20 trillion of debts, and with further pandemic stimulus expected for its economy, it will only be a matter of time when it will collapse by its increasing debts. A slight increase in interest rates will cause severe financial strains to finance its debts. Its policy of quantitative easing will only cause its dollars to weaken further and cause loss of confidence in its currency.

The introduction of digital currency will further erode the usage of the reserve currency and gradually reduce international usage. And in matter of years with the advent of electric cars, the usage of petrol for motor vehicles will gradually be diminished or eliminated. This will have a huge impact on the US dollar where the trading of oil in the international market is in the dollar currency. Any downturn in demand or the total replacement of oil usage with electric consumption will mean the redundancy of US dollar for international transactions.

To add further to US's pains is the maintenance of its over seven hundred military bases spread around the world. This humongous bill for maintaining all these military bases will inevitably put a strain on its economy and also not forgetting its frequent forage in wars in Iraq, Afghanistan, Libya, and Syria will all take a heavy toll in its overall expenditure.

It doesn't take a genius to see that it will only be a matter of time when US economy will collapse on its own reckless spending spree where its expenditure far exceeds that of its revenue. So far it has been able to sustain its deficit and reckless spending because of its reserve currency. But when this crutch is no longer available and further printing of its money is no longer an option, then the crash of the US economy will be inevitable.

China Ramps Up a War of Words, Warning the US of Its Red Lines

As the United States and Taiwan draw closer, state propaganda is sending the message that China will go to war if necessary.

A clip originally posted on the Weibo microblogging platform by the People's Liberation Army's Eastern Theater Command.

By Steven Lee Myers
Published: October 5, 2020; Updated October 6, 2020

Chinese State Media Reacts to Biden Victory with Cautious Optimism

As China's Propaganda Push Continues, Wuhan Emerges as a Star

Diplomacy

Why China's Hopes for a Reset in Relations with US May Be in Vain

- Overtures to the incoming Biden administration are unlikely to be enough to overcome the growing distrust on both sides

- Some diplomatic observations believe concrete measures—such as reopening consulates—will be needed

Macroscope by Anthony Rowley

China's Economic Rise Is Unstoppable – The US Should Explore a Partnership Instead

- China is advancing as an economic power no matter what the US throws at it. This demands a response of acceptance and partnership rather than destructive opposition

Military

China Boosts Nuclear Strike Capability in Face of Growing Rivalry with US, Report Says

- The Bulletin of Atomic Scientists estimates that the PLA has increased the number of ballistic missile brigades by around a third
- Study also estimates that country has around 350 nuclear warheads, most designed for land-based missiles

Who's a 'Bad Actor' on the World Stage?

Washington says it's China but, from arms control to human rights, America poses a far greater threat

By Alex Lo
Published: 9:05 p.m., June 16, 2020

Why you can trust SCMP

102

Alex Lo has been a *Post* columnist since 2012, covering major issues affecting Hong Kong and the rest of China. A journalist for twenty-five years, he has worked for various publications in Hong Kong and Toronto as a news reporter and editor. He has also lectured in journalism at the University of Hong Kong.

My Take

Diplomacy

Empty Seats, Underwhelming Crowd as Trump Attempts Campaign Reboot at Tulsa Rally

Trump Team Blames Protesters After Enormous Crowd for President's First Rally in Months Failed to Materialize

Judge Also Rules Ex-Adviser Bolton Can Publish Tell-All Book Despite Trump Efforts to Block It

By Robert Delaney
Published: 9:41 a.m., June 21, 2020

China

European Union Leaders Urge Xi Jinping to Drop Hong Kong National Security Law, or Risk 'Negative Consequences'

'China Risks Very Negative Consequences' If It Imposes National Security Law, Says European Commission President Ursula Von Der Leyen

But she sidesteps questions as to the exact measures the EU would take.

Chinese President Xi Jinping meets with European Council President Charles Michel and European Commission President Ursula von der Leyen via video link in Beijing on Monday. Photo: Xinhua

European Union leaders warned President Xi Jinping of "very negative consequences" over Beijing's plan to introduce a national security law in Hong Kong, while pressing for progress on market access and climate change in a sign of Europe's hardening approach to China.

But she sidestepped questions as to the exact measures the EU would take.

Why We'll Only See the Full Draft of Hong Kong's National Security Law After It Kicks In

June 23, 2020

Every 12 Minutes, the United States Drops a Bomb Somewhere

by Michael Tennant
Published: June 26, 2018

The United States, which is not legally at war with a single foreign country, is dropping bombs on foreigners at the astounding rate of 121 bombs per day—one bomb every 12 minutes. Worse still, most of the victims of these bombs are not the intended targets. And even worse, the news media, which harps.

US AND OTHER COUNTRIES DECOUPLING FROM CHINA

As early as 1988, China took advantage of its cheap labor by importing raw materials and exporting finished products to rich western economies. This strategic move turned China into a huge global manufacturing hub. This export-oriented strategy made China from an economic backwater to a humongous manufacturing powerhouse.

However, with the fallout from the coronavirus, supply chain bringing manufactured products from China was severely disrupted. With the subsequent lockdown and close borders, and disruption of manufactured products, the supply chain to the other economies came to a standstill.

Initially, export of goods was disrupted, but once China brought the pandemic under control, the situation was reversed. The other economies were struggling with the pandemic and thus China export was curtailed.

And for many foreign companies with a manufacturing base in China, the immediate impulse was to move their supply chain to other countries in the Southeast Asia region, like Vietnam and Thailand. However, it was easier said than done. Many of those companies, despite being given incentives in the form of subsidies to move back to their own country or to another Asian country, were reluctant to make the shift. Japan and South Korea gave financial package for their companies to move their factories to their own country. But still many of these countries did not take the offer. There were various factors that made them reluctant to move away from the Chinese market.

China has a large pool of educated and well-trained labor force which made it easy for them to hire. The infrastructure and mobility of their finished goods to the export and domestic markets were good. And lastly, the 400 million urban middle class in the domestic market created an instant market for their finished goods. With the pros to stay more than the cons to move, it was not surprising that many companies including those from the US were reluctant to decouple. Tim Cook, the boss of Apple said:

"The number one reason why we like to be in China is the people. China has extraordinary skills. And the part that's the most unknown is there's almost two million application developers in China that write apps for the iOS App Store. These are some of the most innovative mobile apps in the world, and the entrepreneurs that run them are some of the most inspiring and entrepreneurial in the world. Those are sold not only here but exported around the world."

"Highly skilled software developers developing apps for the App Store are one reason Apple likes to be in China. But the depth of highly skilled labor in the manufacturing space is why Apple makes its iPhones there."

"China has moved into very advanced manufacturing, so you find in China the intersection of craftsman kind of skill, and sophisticated robotics and the computer science world. That intersection, which is very rare to find anywhere, that kind of skill, is very important to our business because of the precision and quality level that we like. The thing that most people focus on if they're a foreigner coming to China is the size of the market, and obviously it's the biggest market in the world in so many areas. But for us, the number one attraction is the quality of the people."

Citing an example of the type of a highly skilled supplier Apple works closely with, Cook talked at length about recently visiting one company that it has collaborated with for several years:

"I visited ICT—they manufacture, among other things, the AirPods for us. When you think about AirPods as a user, you might think it couldn't be that hard because it's really small. The AirPods have several hundred components in them, and the level of precision embedded into the audio quality—without getting into really nerdy engineering—it's really hard. And it requires a level of skill that's extremely high."

And the idea that Apple simply hands over the design to a company like ICT, which just manufacturers according to spec, is simply untrue, says Cook:

"It's not designed and sent over—that sounds like there's no interaction. The truth is, the process engineering and process development associated with our products require innovation in and of itself. Not only the product but the way that it's made, because we want to make things in the scale of hundreds of millions, and we want the quality level of zero defects. That's always what we strive for, and the way that you get there, particularly when you're pushing the envelope in the type of materials that you have, and the precision that your specifications are forcing, requires a kind of hand-in-glove partnership. You don't do it by throwing it over the chasm. It would never work. I can't imagine how that would be."

Addressing the designed-in-California, made-in-low-cost-China impression that many people have—an impression reinforced by the tagline that is printed on every box containing a new iPhone—Cook had this to say:

"There's a confusion about China. The popular conception is that companies come to China because of low labor cost. I'm not sure what part of China they go to, but the truth is China stopped being the low-labor-cost country many years ago. And that is not the reason to come to China from a supply point of view. The reason is because of the skill, and the quantity of skill in one location and the type of skill it is."

And China has an abundance of skilled labor unseen elsewhere, says Cook:

"The products we do require really advanced tooling, and the precision that you have to have, the tooling and working with the materials that we do are state of the art. And the tooling skill is very deep here. In the US, you could have a meeting of tooling engineers and I'm not sure we could fill the room. In China, you could fill multiple football fields."

Cook credits China's vast supply of highly skilled vocational talent:

"The vocational expertise is very, very deep here, and I give the education system a lot of credit for continuing to push on that even when others were de-emphasizing vocational. Now I think many countries in the world have woke up and said this is a key thing and we've got to correct that. China called that right from the beginning."

This article also appeared on LinkedIn.

The above statement by Tim Cook probably sums up that decoupling manufacturing from China will not be an easy task for those companies that have roots in China.

https://www.scmp.com/week-asia/economics/article/3083988/leave-china-no-thanks-some-japanese-firms-say-tokyos-cash

- Toyota is among the firms who say they have no plans to change their strategy in China, as Tokyo offers subsidies to encourage supply chain diversification
- But leaving the world's second biggest economy isn't going to be that easy or desirable

COVID-19 FROM WUHAN, THE PANDEMIC

The Covid-19 virus was detected in public in late December 2019 in Wuhan, Hubei Province. The people infected at the Hunan Seafood Wholesale Market started to catch pneumonia with an unknown virus.

As of October 2020, according to John Hopkins University, more than 48 million had been infected, 1.2 million deaths, 34 million had been cured for which there is currently no specific treatment or a safely confirmed vaccine although there are several under phase 3 testing.

Initially, the medical team in Wuhan could not determine what it was and generally there was some confusion. This was unfairly criticized by Western media as attempt to hide, delay, and obfuscate data of the virus. Since Wuhan was the first place to be infected with the virus, there was no protocol for it to deal with the surge in the virus. However, when it became clear that it was infectious and possibly transmitted from human to human, notice of the virus was immediately conveyed to the WHO.

However, China was unfairly criticized for the delay in reporting the outbreak. Initially, when the virus was reported, Trump himself heaped lavish praise on the Chinese for doing an excellent job in tackling the virus. The compliment was also given by the DG of WHO in the manner in which the Chinese was able to provide the genome of the virus to scientists all over the world.

However, despite the early warning, US and the European countries could not manage the pandemic, thus resulting in heavy loss of lives. The huge number of daily infections placed a heavy strain on the hospitalization facilities.

By July, China's strict lockdown measures which initially received rebuke from the Western countries began to show signs of controlling the spread of the virus. However, in the US and Europe, the virus spiraled out of control, and from New York, the virus began spreading rapidly from state to state. In Europe, Italy, France, Spain, Germany, and all the EU countries began experiencing increase in the daily infections. Failure to mandate the using of masks and social distancing from the beginning caused the heavy spike of viral infections.

China's success in controlling the virus was not acknowledged by the US and the European countries. Instead of following the protocol that China had adopted, US and the European countries instead refused to mandate the wearing of masks and adopt social distancing. Instead, US under Trump kept on blaming China for the virus and threatened to seek monetary compensation for the origin of the virus which resulted in the pandemic.

What is most unfortunate was that despite China's success in controlling the virus, US and the rest refused to learn from China on how to tackle the pandemic. There is no doubt that China's emphasis on rapid and thorough testing of the population was very successful in detecting and isolating the people infected with the virus. The result speaks for itself, and by August, Wuhan was virtually free of the Covid-19 virus.

Sadly, this was not the case with US and Europe which was now faced with a second wave of infections which was increasing on a daily basis.

As of November, US, UK, and Europe was faced with a dramatic surge in a second wave of infections which appears to spiral out of control.

By November 5, 2020, based on John Hopkins University figure, there were 48 million worldwide infections, 1.2 million deaths, and 34 million cured cases.

Although the US had known about the pandemic in January, the Trump administration failed to make adequate preparations for the pandemic. As a result, many states in the US were caught without face masks, PPE suits, and ventilators. And because there was no clear plan by the federal government, many states were left to look for their own supply of medical equipment.

It is interesting to note that US has been calling to investigate China on the origin of the Covid-19. But when a hundred countries including China signed an agreement (proposed by the EU) to investigate the origin of the virus globally, US declined to sign the agreement. Why? US has a biolab in Fort Detrick, Maryland, and sometime in July, the CDC gave orders to close Fort Detrick. Sometime in July during a Senate hearing, Robert Redfield, the CDC director, admitted a sizable portion of flu deaths was diagnosed as due to Coronavirus. So was there a leakage of some virus from Fort Detrick which caused the unexplained death due to coronavirus? Could this be the reason why the US refused to sign the agreement to investigate the origin of the Covid-19? All these have not been fully investigated and until today have remained a mystery.

In addition, there was a conspiracy theory that the US sent infected soldiers participating the October army game held in Wuhan. The group of soldiers participating stayed near the Wuhan fish market and was seen frequenting the place. Five of their soldiers were struck with a pneumonia-like flu and instead of seeking medical treatment in Wuhan was immediately flown back to the States. Request by the medical authorities for the medical record of the soldiers met with no response.

The acrimonious allegation against China continued unabated, and there were even calls by US lawmakers to sue China for monetary compensation.

Maybe it was poetic justice that by August China was almost totally free of the virus whereas US, UK, and the rest of Europe were experiencing a second wave of attack by the pandemic.

Further reading materials can be obtained from the following sites.

More than 100 countries, including China, have signed the agreement proposed by the EU to investigate the source of the COVID-19 globally. Why does the United States refuse to sign the agreement?

Updated: August 7, 2020

US Touted COVID-19 Cure, Remdesivir, Fails WHO Trials as US Confirmed Cases Surge Past 8M

By Hu Yuwei and Lin Xiaoyi
Source: *Global Times*
Published: October 17, 2020, 17:09:16
Last Updated: October 17, 2020, 17:39:37

Accusing China of COVID-19 'Cover-Up' Is Merely Politics
https://newswav.com/video/V2007_Pp4yXr?s=F_OqrT0Ev

THE IMMINENT COLLAPSE OF
THE AMERICAN EMPIRE

Many may not see the imminent doom of the US Empire. The last days of the American empire is fast approaching and many are in a state of denial. The current US Secretary of State Mike Pompeo has been going round the globe calling China a global threat to peace. But if truth be told, it's not China but the US that is a threat to global peace. The three issues that have been in the crosshair of US ire have been the Taiwan issue, the Hong Kong Security Law, and the China's claim of the nine-dash line in the South China Sea.

The first two issues in fact and in reality have really no basis for any anger or protestation by the US or any of the Western countries.

First, let us deal with Taiwan. Historically, culturally, and whatever standard of yardstick you like to measure, the inescapable fact remains that Taiwan is an unalienable part of China. It is undeniably a territory of China and that was already recognized by the United Nations when China was admitted as a member of the organization. Taiwan until today is not a member of the United Nations for the simple reason that it is recognized as a part of China. If it is part of China, why is the US inciting Taiwan to rebel against China? Why is it selling arms to Taiwan ostensibly to fight against China? If US had no ill-conceived notion of causing Taiwan to rebel against China. why is it stirring and destabilizing the relations between China and Taiwan deemed as part of its territory? The only conclusion is that the US is deliberately inciting Taiwan to break away from China to become an independent state. If that is the US's wet dream, then they would be disappointed. For China, reuniting Taiwan with its motherland is a core issue that China will not compromise. If indeed shove comes to push. China will not hesitate to go to war in defense of that principle.

As a responsible and trustworthy leader, the US should show leadership and honor to encourage the peaceful reunification of Taiwan and China and not encouraging a separation or independence that would have disastrous consequences. But events lately have ended in deliberately provoking China to ignite a military conflict. Not only the Trump administration sent the health minister to Taiwan, but the Senate passed a bill to sell $1.8 billion worth of arms to a renegade province of China. These events are not incidental but are deliberate provocations to perhaps force China to engage in a military conflict.

The second issue is with Hong Kong. Why are the US and the other Western countries making a fuss of China passing a security law in Hong Kong? Historically, is Hong Kong not a territory of China until it was forcibly taken away by the UK government under the Unequal Treaty in 1942? If sovereignty belongs to China, why are countries like the US and UK poking their nose into Beijing's internal affairs? Is that not against international norms that one should not be interfering in the affairs of another country? How would the US and UK respond if China was to interfere in their domestic affairs? Even as recent as the 2016 US Elections, there were already allegations of Russian interference in their presidential election which led to Donald Trump's impeachment. So if the US doesn't want and allow other countries to interfere in their internal affairs, then why are they now interfering in China's internal affairs? Obviously this is double standard and sheer hypocrisy on the part of the US.

Third, US calling China's aggression in the South China Sea by their claim of the nine-dash line. A neutral observer can see that the aggressor is US and not China. Why? The waterways fronting China is the South China Sea, as its very name imply. What is US, a country located in the Gulf of Mexico 6,000 miles away, doing in the South China Sea? Why are they bringing their armada of warships, destroyers, aircraft carriers to the South China Sea? Is that not a way of intimidation to China? They have no legitimate excuse to be sailing in somebody's territory and accusing the other person as the aggressor. China has never prevented commercial navigation in the South China Sea. So why is US bringing their armada of warships under the pretext that it was to protect freedom of navigation? What to protect when there was no blockade in the first place to deny freedom of navigation? That is a flimsy excuse when the actual reason was to look for a fight.

The world reality situation is that the US is the biggest warmongering nation. Its war on terror since 2001 has injured and displaced millions across twenty-four nations. Its military budget is 40 percent of the global total. On the other hand, China has only waged one war with Vietnam in 1979 in the past fifty years. The US has been in a perpetual state of war for the last two decades. Its war on terror since September 11 has displaced 37 million of people from Pakistan, Afghanistan, Iraq, Yemen, Libya, and Syria. Jimmy Carter, the former president, noted that the US was "the most warlike nation in the history of the world" only at peace for sixteen years of its history. Despite Mike Pompeo's claim, US is the warmongering nation and not China.

For China, going to war against the US is not an option. It would be a foolhardy choice. China has spent the last forty years building its nation. It has uplifted 700 million of its rural people from poverty, and by 2020, it expects to uplift another 50 million. China does not export its ideology, and it would be a surprise if any country would aspire to adopt its version. Its economic model of socialism with Chinese characteristic is working well for its one-party system. And it does not harbor any ambition to adopt the liberal democratic model of the US. But US is fearful of peer competition.

No matter what China does, US will still have to push China down. If Graham Allison's Thucydides theory hold water, a current global power will not tolerate any emerging power out to dethrone him. So it does not really matter even if China was to adopt the US constitutional system or its liberal democracy. US will still not accept any peer competition and will find ways to destroy that competitor.

On November 8, 2020 when the twenty electoral college votes from Pennsylvania was given to Joe Biden, he was finally declared as the forty-sixth president-elect. Despite the celebratory mood that ensued by Biden's presidential victory, the reality of the occasion was that Biden had inherited a divided nation.

The shocking truth that confronted the nation was how did this liberal democratic country elected a forty-fifth president who was a bankrupt six times, who lied daily, and at last count yielded 20,000 lies; someone by his own confession had grabbed the female genitalia, and committed fornication with prostitutes, and in the process married and divorced four times could even be elected the president of this country. And what has even brought more disrepute to this country is that in the contest for his second term, this man, this despicable man could still garner 70 million people to vote for him. And what does it say for this country, the US of America? This can only spell doom for this country.

Not only does Biden has to heal and unite a divided nation, but a world on the threshold of seeing a battle between a current power and an emerging power, China. But Graham Allison's Thucydides theory need not come to fruition if Biden could steer the US to one of cooperation to one of confrontation. China has not gone to war for forty years and it does not look for one now, and if Biden can bring the two nations together through peaceful cooperation, there is still a prospect for the two nations to work for the betterment of the world.

Donald Trump Won, No Matter What Happens Next This Election Showed Us the Real America (Again)

That's America. One gigantic disappointment.
The Apeiron Blog
By Jessica Wildfire

President Putin Floats the Idea of A Russia-China Military Alliance, and the US Isn't Impressed
Published: October 25, 2020, by financetwitter

THE FUTURE OF CHINA

The future of China will hinge on its next five-year blueprint. It will no longer be predicated on who is elected to be the next president of America, either Donald Trump or Joe Biden. The bipartisan policies are too embedded in US strategic thinking and this is unlikely to change. The Pentagon and the US State Department have already designated China's threat to America's global hegemony and have already plotted various measures to weaken China's progress. Trump's initial tariffs on China's exports were just the beginning, and this was followed by a ban on supply chain of chips for China's tech giant Huawei.

By now, China should already realized they can no longer depend on their old model of relying on export to various countries which through US plodding has now become hostile. Even EU countries have been considering a strategic bloc with the new US administration to confront China's assertive posture. India and US together with Japan and Australia have also formed the Quad Alliance to confront China.

Under such a hostile environment facing China, and with US sanctions, tariffs, and export controls that could deter and delay economic development, China has to now device a shift in its focus to "integrating and assimilating" foreign innovations to domestic innovations.

China's new five-year plan embodies the "dual circulation" concept. This concept basically divides the strategy into an internal and external circulation. The internal circulation precipitates on the expansion of growth through domestic consumption, whereas the external circulation refers to the foreign trade economy. The primary focus of the policy is to place more emphasis on homegrown technology to avoid placing heavy reliance on foreign technology and concurrently funded by high-quality exports.

The emphasis is a more inward-looking policy that will no longer depend on the old growth model of heavy reliance on export. The current international backlash from the pandemic and hostile attitude from India and Australia further cement China's resolve to focus more on its domestic growth fueled principally by the resurgence of its 400 million middle class.

US should stop trying to change China's socialist system with Chinese characteristic to that of a liberal democracy. China is quite happy with its present governing structure which has brought immense success to its economy. And China has not attempted to export its ideology to any countries. In fact, it would be surprised if there were any country willing to adopt its system. The reality is that the Chinese system is easily adapted to China's form of governance because the Chinese psyche of obedience to authority is culturally embedded in the Chinese minds. Also historically china's governance has always been one based on meritocracy, and because of such a policy, the people in office are experienced and well qualified. Unlike the American system where you can change the party but you cannot change the policy, China's situation is just the reverse where you can change the policy but you cannot change the party. The merit of such a policy is that all policies are swiftly and efficiently implemented without going through endless red tape as the case in a democratic government.

US ban on the supply chain to China's high-tech company will not provide an obstacle to China's march to be the biggest economy in GDP terms in ten years' time. At most it will slow China's progress but realistically will not stop China from overtaking the US as world's top economy.

Newly elected President-elect Joe Biden would make a calculated mistake by assuming an allies bloc consisting of the Five Eyes alliance (UK, Canada, Australia, and New Zealand) and the EU could form an effective coalition in stomping China's economic progress. China's market of 1.4 billion people is twice that of the US and EU combined, and all China has to do is to cut off the supply chain of exports to these Western countries and you will see the downward trajectory of their respective GDP growth. China's previous and existing export oriented market has spurred economic growth in these countries, and the sudden deprivation of access to China's export and import market would create a vacuum no country could supplant. This would be an unmitigated disaster for these countries so used to the cheap imports and reliance on Chinese products and a vast market for their exports.

Instead of a confrontationist policy adopted by previous US administration, Biden would do the US and the rest of the world a big favor by a policy of engagement with China. Collaborations in all aspect of trade, technology, innovations, medical (vaccine), and space technology would ensure peace and future prosperity for all mankind. Its current policy of demonizing and destabilizing China by creating conflicts in Taiwan, Hong Kong, Xinjiang, and the South China Seas will only result in a military conflict that will only engulf the region and the world in a disastrous world war that would only result in the destruction of this planet.

US's current administration should seriously appraise the possibility of a military conflict in the Southeast Asia region caused by an unexpected error of judgement that could trigger a serious conflict between the two superpowers. And if push comes to shove, US would be foolish to expect China to be a walkover invasion like it did in Iraq, Afghanistan, and Libya. If US cannot defeat China in 1945 when the latter was using sticks and stones to fight US and Allied forces in Korea which led to the truce demarcated by the 39th parallel between North and South Korea, what chance does it have of defeating a China well equipped with modern weapons? It would be a colossal mistake for the US to think it could cause another era of humiliation to China after the last century of humiliations which the Chinese had endured in the past.

In summary, I have to emphasize that China does not seek to be a hegemony global power. Its historical past certainly proves it. In its forty years of economic development, it has not engaged in wars (except in 1979 with Vietnam) unlike the US which has been constantly engaged in war in its two hundred years of hegemony power.

China's current global expansion does not involve militarism nor colonization like all the previous imperialists powers of United Kingdom, Germany, France, Japan, and the US. Its Belt and Road Initiative encompasses the building of infrastructure to bring development and prosperity on the concept of a vision of shared prosperity for all nations. Its vision of shared prosperity for all participating nations should be applauded not demonized by Western nations.

Reference: Further articles from various post can be read from site below.

China Economy

China's Asean Influence Sets Stage for New Superpower Battleground with US, as the Ball Shifts to Biden's Court

- In America's absence, China has been strengthening its economic hand in Southeast Asia, while the region is becoming increasingly important amid trade disputes
- But 'incorrigible hedgers' in Asean do not want to become pawns in a geopolitical game between the world's largest economies

REPORT
US. Security Policy in Asia: Implications for China-US Relations
Wu Xinbo
Published: September 1, 2000

ASIA GEOPOLITICS | DIPLOMACY | RISK INTELLIGENCE | SECURITY | EAST ASIA

China and the Coming Biden Presidency

How will US President-elect Joe Biden manage the US-China relationship?

By Ankit Panda
Published: November 14, 2020

CHINA POWER | DIPLOMACY | EAST ASIA

Why Hasn't China Congratulated Joe Biden?

China is keeping its head low for the simple reason that it has nothing to gain by doing anything different.

By Shannon Tiezzi
Published: November 10, 2020

THE CHINESE ARE LEAVING US IN THE DUST

https://documentoud.adobe.com/link/review?uri=urn:aaid:scd
s:US:9ca76ea5-5e76-48de-b359-902d81c7015c#pageNum=1cl

AN INTERNET SURVEY OF RECENT CHINESE ACHIEVEMENTS

By Jim Gordon

1. Railways
2. Dams
3. Ports
4. Bridges
5. Roads
6. Airports
7. Aircrafts
8. Space
9. Miscellaneous Statistics